Africa Rising:
Shedding Black Africa's Burden

By
David Ogula

First published by Dog Ear Publishing
4011 Vincennes Rd
Indianapolis, IN 46268
www.dogearpublishing.net

ISBN: 978-0-578-52412-2

Library of Congree Control Number: 2017953610

This book is printed on acid-free paper.

Printed in the United States of America

Contents

Dedication

To my children and all African children
who deserve a better future without the
burdens presented herein.

Acknowledgement

This project was made possible by the support of many people: family members and friends. Without their support this project would have remained unfulfilled. I owe a debt of gratitude to my colleagues and friends with whom I shared my thoughts, and struggles during the different phases of writing this manuscript. I would like to thank Emily Rahimi for helping to proof read my manuscript and all my friends for their suggestions, encouragement and guidance.

Preface

Change in the world today is accelerating at an alarming pace; driven by continuous innovation and almost infinite possibilities. Traditional and geopolitical firewalls that separated people in self-contained entities have all but collapsed. Technology and innovation have allowed a free flow of information, making it possible for nations large and small to craft solutions to human problems. The wave of change has influenced reconstruction of social, legal, economic and political systems. As Thomas Friedman noted, in *The World is Flat: A Brief History of the - twenty-first Century,* people living in developed nations no longer have the playing field tilted in their favor. Increasingly, enterprising individuals based in India, China, or Brazil have the same opportunities to better themselves as those living in Western Europe, the United States, or Canada. Human advancement in the twenty-first century is no longer dictated by a handful of nations as technology has opened up endless possibilities for trade, collaboration and invention.

These sweeping changes force one to ask if change is happening upon Africa or Africans are driving and directing the changes occurring in the continent. Nonetheless, the torrents of change have not bypassed Africa. The wireless communication revolution sweeping across the globe has immensely benefited Africa. Almost all corners of the continent today have been connected with wireless communications technology.

The position taken in this book is one that sees Africans shaping the course of change not as passive actors, but active agents. Africa in the twenty-first century must shed the image of impoverishment and decline evident in black communities in developed and developing countries. They must create thriving cultures that foster innovation, creativity, economic prosperity, and growth. Africa must shed its appetite for the passive consumption of finished products from the rest of the world. Only then can black Africans raise their chins high and say they have come of age and are contributing to human progress.

Introduction

"Africa, my Africa of proud warriors in ancestral savannahs
Africa of whom my grandmother sings
On the banks of the distant river I have never known you
But your blood flows in my veins
Your beautiful black blood that irrigates the fields
The blood of your sweat
The sweat of your work
The work of your slavery"
David Diop. "Africa."

Africa is the second largest continent in population and size, spanning 30,065,000 square kilometers or 11,608,161 square miles, and inhabited by approximately one billion people. This large population is by no means monolithic, comprising a glorious mix of cultures and ethnicities, and a complex array of political and economic systems. But despite their differences, black Africans share many of the same burdens and aspirations—to enjoy individual freedoms, political self-determination, good governance, and lasting peace; to benefit from basic health care, clean drinking water, and decent roads; and to eradicate preventable diseases, hunger, and illiteracy. Unfortunately, these basic human desires remain unfulfilled for the vast majority of black Africans living today.

The African continent is richly endowed with abundant natural resources that have been exploited to the benefit of many nations, corporations and individuals; but black Africans have profited little from this wealth. Paradoxically, the African countries that are most richly endowed with natural resources often have the highest rates of poverty. It can be argued that mismanagement of oil wealth in major producers,

1

such as Angola, Equatorial Guinea, Nigeria, Sao Tome and Sudan has played a substantial role in the ruinous human development record of these countries. To realize the promise of prosperity in the twenty-first century, black African nations must learn to exploit their natural resources for the benefit of their own citizens, and the advancement of the continent as a whole.

For over a century, external forces have driven the agenda for progress and development throughout black Africa. Control has been exerted during the colonial and post-colonial periods through the imposition of policies formulated by foreign governments, transnational corporations, non-governmental organizations (NGOs), and religious and humanitarian organizations. African leaders who may not have fully grasped the implications and potential complications of such policies enthusiastically embraced the proposed programs, only to abandon them, leaving behind a trail of shattered dreams.

During the past half-century, the United Nations and wealthy Western countries have contributed millions of dollars in aid to help alleviate Africa's problems, but the inadequacies of this foreign-driven approach are evident in African communities where the aid has had a negligible impact. Often donations are made through NGOs in response to humanitarian disasters caused by war, ethnic conflicts, disease and famine, but the resources offered do not always reach the people they are intended to help, particularly those in isolated rural villages. Furthermore, the injection of millions of dollars in aid often creates false expectations, a sense of entitlement, and a mentality of dependence on foreign intervention.

Some have argued that aid programs are based on grossly misaligned objectives, and that development initiatives formulated abroad may not take into account either local needs or the complex interactions among various ethnic groups. Others point to corrupt government officials and their cronies, who may divert aid money for personal use. Wherever the faults may lie, there is an urgent need to look beyond temporary crisis relief in Africa, and to build broad-based internal support for lasting development.

Many African citizens today are seeking a new approach, with direct involvement in the process of transforming their own countries and lives. They want to tackle the problems of infrastructural underdevelopment, lack of economic growth, and insufficient trade and investments. They are hungry for real progress that will transform not only their physical environment, but also the social, political and economic frameworks that support their endeavors. With the example of democratic and progressive societies around the world to guide and inspire them, they wish to become masters of their own destiny.

The first part of this book takes a look in the mirror approach; it explores black Africa's burdens, which have impeded the renaissance of the entire continent despite vast expenditures of financial and human capital in the interest of social, cultural and economic development. The concept of an African consciousness or refined African phenomenology in the twenty-first century, and the social fragmentation experienced by black Africans—even those in the diaspora—which has constrained the unity of purpose required to build a progressive path forward, and the absence of a disciplined and focused approach to solving present problems will be discussed. The roots of this impasse lie buried deep in black Africa's past. This destructive cycle perpetuated by a failure of modern leadership to join forces in the name of progress for all of black Africa, creates negative consequences for black people living and striving throughout the global community.

The second part of this book lays a course of action to place black Africa on the path to sustainable development. Urgent steps for the reconstruction of black African culture and society and for preparing black Africans to compete in the modern global economy will be proffered and ideas to imprint a vision of success and innovation that will shape black Africa's common future for generations will be proposed. The ideas discussed are by no means exhaustive, but they will provide a roadmap and a way forward for development that could set the standard for the social, cultural, and economic revitalization of black people and nations around the world.

PART

I

The Black Burden

If we tell, gently, gently
All that we shall one day have to tell,
Who then will hear our voices without laughter,
Sad complaining voices of beggars
Who indeed will hear them without laughter?
If we roughly of our torments
Ever increasing from the start of things
What eyes will watch our large mouths
Shaped by the laughter of big children
What eyes will watch our large mouth?
What hearts will listen to our clamoring?
What ear to our pitiful anger
Which grows in us like a tumor
In the black depth of our plaintive throats?

Kwesi Brew, "Vanity."

Human societies have always struggled to cope with the challenges of adapting to changing conditions and new technologies, and this creative driving force has shaped the course of human progress. As industrialized nations forge ahead with technological advances once thought impossible, and nations around the globe strive to overcome the challenges of the modern industrialized world, most black African communities seem mired in cycles of conflict and political instability, poverty and hunger, disease, widespread illiteracy, rampant crime, economic dependency, and infrastructural underdevelopment. Africa in the twenty-first century remains a continent viewed with pity or contempt, its people seen as helplessly gazing beyond the horizons or toward the heavens for a savior who does not come.

The cumulative weight of these heavy burdens has raised serious concerns about black Africa's ability to develop the sophisticated mechanisms required for civilization to thrive in the modern world. Many wonder why Africa has experienced no age of reformation or enlightenment, as Europe did in centuries ago? Why has Africa been plagued by enduring famine and poverty despite its abundant natural resources? And why have Africans been unable to create their own formula for societal transformation and development?

Black Africa's complex developmental problems can be attributed to a combination of historical and cultural factors. Though experts may disagree about the relative weight of various influences, there is general consensus about the range of issues contributing to the current unpromising state of affairs.

Black Africa today – What the data shows

To demonstrate the urgency of lifting the black burden, a frank assessment of the challenges faced by black African nations today must be made. By every measure of human achievement and quality of life, black Africa is at the lowest levels compared to almost all other regions of the world. While some black African countries have performed better than others, and many individuals achieve a high level of education and professional success, a majority of black Africans struggle to survive before they can hope to strive for personal achievement and the opportunities available to them are severely limited.

A few vital statistics reveal the stark contrasts between Sub-Saharan Africa and the United States of America, as evidence of the developmental chasm that separates the world's most powerful nation from the most destitute region on earth:

Data Point	Sub-Saharan Africa	United States of America
Average life expectancy	54.2 years (2010)	78.2 years (2010)
Infant mortality rate	69.4 per 1,000 live births (2011)	6.4 per 1,000 live births (2011)
Births attended by	46.1% (2010)	99.3% (2003) skilled health staff
Literacy (adult,	62.6% (2010)	99.99% (2008) [1] age 15 and above)
School enrollment	6.8% (2011)	94.8% (2010) tertiary (% gross) [higher education]
Internet users	12.3 (2011)	78.2 (2011) (per 100 people)
Access to electricity	32.4% (2009)	100% (2000) [2]

All figures from data.worldbank.org, except as indicated.

[1] CIA World Factbook
[2] Based on IEA (International Energy Agency), World Energy Outlook (from Unesco.org).

The enormity of the problem is daunting, as facilities and services lack in many crucial areas, and too few young Africans have been provided with the professional skills required to address these concerns. Without unified action from government and community leaders, as well as black African professionals on the continent and abroad, there is little hope for narrowing the gaps that separate black Africa from the rest of the world—gaps that seem wider and deeper than the oceans surrounding the beautiful, ancient continent.

Adrift in a modern world?

Time and geology have shaped the African continent and its people; Africa is a place where the thread of ancient civilization remains deeply woven into the fabric of modern daily life. This enduring bond to the distant past can be seen as Africa's unique strength, but it is also one of its most dangerous weaknesses. Africa's resources and strength should be a source of pride and dignity for all black people. Instead, the Africans' view of themselves sharply contradicts its place in the modern world.

The images of modern day Africa paints a stunning irony between that sense of pride that streams from Africa's status as the font of human civilization and its inability to build that sense of pride to better the lives of its people. The challenge is for black Africa to take responsibility for its own development, without allowing its primal proclivities to take control. Few black Africans feel truly proud of their place in the modern world, which seems to have left them behind in almost every aspect of human development- from technological development to providing the basic needs of daily life. The primal energy of African culture stirs the imagination of people in every other corner of the world, but it seems at odds with modern existence, which is characterized by technological innovation, increasing urbanization, and democratic and pluralistic governance. With its roots sunk deep in her prehistoric heritage, one is compelled to ask, can black Africa rise to meet the challenges of the Space Age? The answer will depend on whether black African leaders, nations and people can learn to carry the riches of the past into the future without letting the burden weigh them down.

Tribalism and superstition – the modern costs

A sense of tribal identity remains almost as strong in modern Africa as it was in the pre-industrial past, though lifestyles have changed dramatically for many Africans, and tribal leadership has largely been superseded by bureaucratic government entities in the Western democratic mold.

On March 28, 2016, at an event accessing the U.S.-Nigeria partnership at the United States Institute of Peace (USIP), a young Nigerian female asked Ambassador Linda Thomas-Greenfield, U.S. Assistant Secretary, Bureau of African Affairs, what the U.S. could do to mitigate the destructive effects of tribalism. Ambassador Thomas-Greenfield's response-that tribalism is a problem Africans have to work through places responsibility on Africans to spearhead solving their own problems. Though strong tribal identity can still allow rural African communities to cohere, it wreaks havoc on efforts to unify black Africans and mobilize them to function in a modern context. Exaggerated tribal loyalty fuels conflicts which impede development programs that benefit diverse communities.

Beliefs rooted in supernatural forces may guide individual and social behavior in every aspect of daily life. Despite the influence of monotheistic religions and modern education, superstitious practices remain prevalent throughout much of black Africa, and their effects can be damaging to individual lives, as well as social development. One well-publicized example is the widespread belief that intercourse with a girl who is a virgin can cleanse the blood of a man infected with AIDS—a superstition that has directly resulted in the rape and infection of countless young African women, and children.

If black Africans are to lift themselves out of poverty and disadvantage, and rise to join the global community, they must examine those aspects of their cultural heritage that are incompatible with 21st century life, and adapt to the contemporary socio-political environment, so that they can embrace the opportunities for development offered in collaboration with intercontinental partners. To win the respect of the global community, black Africa must prove itself capable of advancing its own development plans. Shedding outmoded superstitious beliefs and tribal loyalties would go a long way in lifting black Africa's burden.

Colonialism and slavery – a trail of cultural negation

It is impossible to overestimate the detrimental social and psychological effects of centuries of domination and exploitation by foreign powers and the enslavement of countless of black Africans as commodities and a source of labor in the homes and fields of the world's more powerful nations. More than a century after the last slaves were freed, and a half-century after the last African colonies gained independence, the residual stigma of racially-based subjugation still scars the hearts of black people around the world, and marks them as inferior in the eyes of some or even in their own distorted view.

Reflecting on the causes of the African burden presents a serious challenge. The first thing that comes to mind is the effect of the experience of slave trade and colonialism on black Africans. One of the responses stimulated by this line of thought, is the claim that the African experience of slavery, colonialism, and neo-colonialism disrupted Africa's ability to chart its own path for development.

European colonizers systematically undermined African culture as a way of disrupting the social structures of native populations, and making them easier to control. They looked down on indigenous cultural traditions, which they saw as primitive and barbaric, and inferior to Western civilization in every way. The historic record of African achievement is fractured and incomplete, due in part to the destructive influence of this cultural collision. Similarly, Africans sold into slavery were cut off from all aspects of their native social and cultural context by slave traders and owners who separated members of tribes and families, abolished African names, and confiscated African musical instruments. Those enslaved had no choice but to assimilate their oppressors' culture, though they also managed to imprint it with their own spirit, enriching the world with new musical forms that are now considered part of the global cultural heritage. But black African slaves also assimilated a damaged image of their own place in the world, which manifests in subtle behaviors oblivious to the black African. Others openly exhibit subservient and inferior behaviors —and this false self-image has stubbornly endured, seemingly reflected back in any mirror held up to contemporary black Africa.

The glories of pre-colonial civilizations such as the empires of Benin, Ghana, Mali, and Songhai are all but forgotten, and largely unknown to the greater world. Lacking detailed historical records of past achievements, modern black Africans and black people on every continent can never point with pride to the evidence of their cultural heritage and birthright; instead, they are marked with a humiliating past and failure to thrive as black African nations that won independence from their colonizers.

The most striking assessment of the evolution of the African burden comes from combining insights from the African experience of slavery and pre- and post-colonialism. Such appraisal allows for examination of intrinsic and extrinsic factors that contributed to stagnation in Africa. This line of analysis not only identifies the influence of the slave trade, colonialism, and neo-colonialism on Africa but also examines Africa's inability to generate an internal impetus for advancement. It adds the view that Africa's burden is as much rooted in its own understanding and constructs of the world. This line of reasoning also attempts to unveil correlations between the African worldview and the black burden.

Limitations to the psychology of blaming external forces and victimhood may be illustrated with a simple, hostile landlord-tenant relationship. A landlord is unlikely to blame a tenant who damaged his property long after the landlord evicted the tenant. If the landlord does nothing and continues to blame the tenant for the damages to his property, decades after taking possession, the landlord's position can hardly be justified.

In addition, Africans who have acquired Western education have failed to integrate their understanding of the past to shape a new path of enlightenment and progress for Africa. Collectively, Africans both educated and uneducated - have failed to utilize their accumulated knowledge for their advancement. They have remained passive consumers of Western discoveries, driven by blind political and economic forces, and have demonstrated an inability to grasp the unremitting winds of change.

The influence of foreign powers on post-colonial African development

In the late 1950s and through the 1960s, African nations began gaining freedom from the shackles of colonialism. Ghana became the first in 1957, followed by Guinea, in 1958, and a host of other African countries in the 1960s: Cameroon, Senegal, Togo, Mali, Somalia, Benin, Niger, Central African Republic, Congo (Brazzaville), Gabon, Nigeria, etc.[1] Independence was herald as the beginning of a new era filled with the hopes and dreams of a prosperous and glorious future. However, despite the transfer of political power, these nations remained economically bound to the colonial powers. The colonial authorities maintained control of mineral resources and agricultural produce. Industrial production was sustained only at the level of processing raw materials for export to the colonial powers – keeping the host nations underdeveloped and the local populations in poverty.

Kwame Nkrumah, the first President of Ghana framed the new burden as "neocolonialism."[2] He described it as the external control and exploitation of post-colonial African nations through economic, political, and cultural means, despite the transfer of power to indigenous governmental bodies. In his view, Africa's colonizers maintained their domination of the continent through multinational corporations, to extract economic and resource value while keeping the populace in a state of dependence and underdevelopment.

The multinational corporations that dominated African economies did little to share profits equitably. Indigenous labor, which was relied upon for production was exploited, paid low wages, marginalized, and kept poor. Investments were made without a real transformative impact on the host countries, and no effort was made to build capacity or place the host nations on the path to self-sufficiency. The underdevelopment of independent African nations was further cemented in the absence of good governance, functioning government institutions, and transparent financial management, and profits from external investments were diverted through corrupt channels and drained from the national economy without providing any substantial benefit to the general public.

Practices such as these kept post-colonial countries in a state of perennial economic subjugation, regardless of the transfer to indigenous political control. The "colonizing" powers and their military may not have been visible on the ground, but they effectively manipulated the economies of developing countries from abroad, while using local labor to create profit at margins of return that would not be possible in developed countries with strong labor laws, higher standards of living, and established social service administrations. Ideally, the benefits from foreign investment would have offset the temporary disadvantages, and injected needed development capital into local economies, but the absence post-colonial industrial development plans hindered progress.

Black African originality – reinventing black creative power

Prior to the modern period of European colonialism, which lasted roughly a century, black African civilization was characterized by numerous widely diverse cultural groups linked through intricate networks of economic and political associations. While some populations were highly centralized with complex political and social structures, others lived in smaller and more isolated or nomadic tribal groups. Despite the obstacles posed by the vast landscape, African goods were widely traded and highly prized abroad due to the fine quality of workmanship in manufactured items, as well as the value of rare commodities such as ivory and gold. Describing the sophistication of African production methods before the 15th century, Alexander Ives Bortolot wrote:

> Contrary to popular views about precolonial Africa, local manu-facturers were at this time creating items of comparable, if not superior, quality to those from preindustrial Europe. Due to advances in native forge technology, smiths in some regions of Sub-Saharan Africa were producing steels of a better grade than those of their counterparts in Europe, and the highly developed West African textile workshops had produced fine cloths for export long before the arrival of European traders.[3]

At this time, the trade in black African slaves was also well established within the continent and beyond.

During the period of intense European colonization in the 19th and 20th centuries, black African societies were subjected to extreme cultural pressures, with the aim of fundamentally reconfiguring their social structure in the image of the colonizing powers.[4] This process was profoundly destructive to indigenous cultures, as the rationalist, individualist European worldview was diametrically opposed to African traditional views, which were perceived as animistic. The communalist spirit of African social groups, which relied on oral tradition to transmit their cultural heritage were also systematically dismantled. Since Africans adopted the languages of the colonizers as the official languages of the colonies, Africans lost the most direct link with their unique cultural identity. It is impossible to determine if lost languages and traditional identities can be reclaimed by Africans now many generations removed from their pre-colonial ancestors.

Thus sundered from the deep roots of its ancient past, black Africa seemed to have lost its originality, the sources of its creative inspiration, and, some may say, its creative soul. But how can modern black Africans hope to challenge current world leaders in technological or scientific innovation and design, when their own cultural identity and sense of self-worth have been so radically depleted, and their societies have been wrenched apart and reconfigured based on alien models imposed by their former conquerors? This question lies at the heart of the African burden, and the answers provided may form the basis for reinventing black Africa's unique ingenuity, and reinvigorating its languishing communities.

It can be argued that the combined effects of slavery, colonialism and neocolonialism have disrupted black Africa's ability to chart its own path for development, by destroying social systems uniquely adapted to the innate character of indigenous peoples and the exigencies of their environment. Some in the West contend that African cultural constructs are inherently primitive and unsuited to the demands of a technologically complex civilization, while others decry the prejudicial stigmatization of African cultures based on Eurocentric standards. But no one can deny that urgent change is required for black African nations to advance on the world stage, and for black Africans to improve their quality of life. If a way forward is to be found, new social and political structures must be built from the ground up, to make the most of African strengths, while avoiding the pitfalls that have impeded progress for decades.

The black African consciousness

Scholars of African history and culture may disagree about the degree to which different factors have impacted the social psychology of post-colonial Africa, but there is no doubt that the cumulative effects have been profound and lasting. A more controversial issue is the concept of a pre-existing, uniquely African consciousness or personality type, and the discussion of how it was formed, how it can be characterized, and how it could affect the prospects for African renewal and success in the modern world.

Malaika Mutere argues that an indigenous African personality has survived, despite concerted attempts to destroy it and assimilate Africans into Western culture.[5] This view not only posits a fundamental difference in African psychology but also implies that in their unique outlook, Africans maintain a reservoir of cultural and personal resilience in the face of oppression by aggressors with opposing worldviews. This argument has many supporters, but is not without detractors among social scientists and other observers of post-colonial development in African nations, or more to the point, the continuing failure to develop in pace with global competitors, negate claims that Africans have overcome their problems.

In a survey of scholarly work on the subject, James E. Lassiter describes the basic conceptual disagreement, and possible implications:

Western social scientists abandoned typical personality and national character studies during the 1960s. However, many Sub-Saharan African scholars in various disciplines, those resident on the continent and elsewhere, have continued to identify, describe and make use of what they consider to be widespread African psychological characteristics and patterns of cultural adaptation. These include core African cultural values and themes, and what the scholars believe are common African responses to the requirements of social life and external cultural influences. To them, the analysis and use of these widely shared values, themes and adaptive responses are crucial for achieving viable and sustainable African national and community development. In fact, a number of the thinkers argue this endeavor is necessary for the ultimate survival of Africa and its cultures. In contrast, Western and non-Western social scientists have given up pursuing such broad concepts and adaptive processes as areas of invalid and/or harmful social science inquiry.[6]

Naturally there are widely divergent views about the subject of black African consciousness, and there is no consensus as to whether the personality traits and attitudes considered by some as uniquely black African constitute an essential element of indigenous culture, a regressive attachment to traditional beliefs, a crippling remnant of historical trauma or some combination of these and other elements.

Misplaced group allegiance

Another burden that hinders progressive advancement among black people is misplaced allegiances that contribute to the perception of a collective lowering of standards. It is often disguised as group unity or supporting the group. Such expression of group affinity is not unique to Africans, but in the context of widespread underdevelopment, it has a damaging impact. The contexts in which terms such as "keeping it real,' "this na Niga O," "African time," "Nigerianietis," "small thing," etc., resonate are often stereotypical or negative. The context in which some blacks "keep it real" is not often in situations of high achievement or accomplishments; it is used to maintain a condition that is abhorrent, dysfunctional, or reinforce a self-affirming stereotype. Community members pressure others to accept or conform to these norms. Generally condoned by the population, it is more insidiously about resistance to progressive change and such social norms engender a culture that perpetuates mediocrity.

The broken spirit of community

African cultures take great pride in their communal tradition based on the belief that cooperation among individuals is for the good of all, and no one can live well without the support of others. The only way to lift up a community or a country is by nourishing this cooperative spirit, with the understanding that helping each one is helping all and this is the basis of human society.

The competitive drive is also a part of human nature, and it can spur black Africans to greater heights in every endeavor. But in too many black African countries, healthy competition among equals with mutual respect is not the norm; instead, those who gain advantages are apt to use their influence to exploit those less fortunate, with no regard for the consequences. Empathy and charity are reserved for the extended family and close friends, and those who lack wealthy connections are doomed to a life of poverty, or even early death. Those who pursue and achieve elite status have too often become a destructive antisocial force, rather than a catalyst for development.

Black African nations are more than discreet neighbors sharing a continent—they are an interdependent web, with diverse cultural groups that often sprawl across semi-porous borders, often reliant upon the same resources, and challenged by the same needs. If the collections of African communities are to prosper, it must be through collaboration and compromise. Time is of the essence, and the bar must be raised for all members of the black African community on the local, national, and international levels, and great things should be expected from all, for the sake of all.

For the purpose of this book, the crucial question is how the attitudes of black Africans affect their chances for advancement in the world today, and what adjustments will be required for successful adaptation to the modern globalized environment.

CHAPTER 2

Black African Phenomenology

"Tradition is the illusion of permanence."
Woody Allen.

Human societies are based on shared beliefs, values, experiences, and other cultural forces that unify the group and provide reference points for the individual participants, so they can make sense of the world they live in and feel a secure pride of place in it. This is the wellspring from which every society draws its sustenance and strength. It can enable a nation to rise from the ashes of cataclysmic disaster, and rebuild in a new image without losing its identity or soul. Black Africans face two fundamental challenges in this regard: Preserving its cultural identity or cleansing aspects that are at odds with the modern world to allow for contemporary technology-based, post-industrial globalized, economic, political, and social structures.

To build forward momentum, the outlook of any social group and the individuals within it must be focused toward the future with hope and enthusiasm, and with confidence in the people's ability to solve their own problems through a cooperative effort. If energies are diverted or drained by regressive, counter-productive attitudes and cultural constructs, it will be impossible to initiate and sustain prolonged development. Transforming black African consciousness will be critical for African progress, because it is the prism through which Africans view and interpret their world, and its clarity and character will determine the success or failure of reconstruction and development.

If foreign oppression has damaged black African consciousness and culture, black Africans in every walk of life, from leaders and elites to the poorest of the poor, have internalized this damaged and warped view of their place in the world, and reinforced its destructive strength. Those in power often reenact the oppressive policies of past colonial masters, and those they oppress feel powerless to challenge or change unjust social and political structures. To some observers, it seems as if black Africans learned all the negative behaviors of their colonizers, without absorbing or adopting the positive elements of Western culture and technology, and adapting them to the African context for their own purposes.

To break this destructive cycle, it will be necessary to initiate a seismic shift in black African consciousness, with the aim of empowering social change on a continental scale. Old habits of self-defeating thought must be uprooted, and minds opened to the possibility of creating a better life.

The African sense of the natural world – at odds with technology-driven progress?

Black African phenomenology draws on an ancient sense of human harmony with nature, and most of the indigenous customs, values, and beliefs are founded on this central organizing principle. From this perspective, the role of humanity is not to tame or control the natural environment, but to integrate organically with it, as part of a unified whole. Chronic underdevelopment in Africa also raises concerns about why African consciousness in relation to nature focuses only on the human connection to nature, but is deficient in the perception that humans "can also transcend nature by progressively mastering it and subduing it."[7]

In black African belief systems, elements of the landscape or environment can be the focus of religious contemplation, and spirits can be thought to inhabit them for good or evil purposes. While this belief system helped to preserve pre-colonial indigenous African values, it also proved a crippling handicap when indigenous Africans were confronted with European cultures that no longer held such beliefs about man's place in the natural order, and saw the undeveloped African continent as a storehouse of resources to be plundered and exploited.

In the modern Western view, man's aim is to master his environment, and make use of all it can offer for his own benefit. Since the dawn of the industrial age and the rise of machine-based technologies, the range of human endeavor on earth has become almost limitless, and our reach has extended beyond our world to probe the depths of space. Developed nations vie with one another to produce the next miraculous discovery that will revolutionize our understanding of the universal forces that shape us all, and improve the way we live our lives. The drive to unravel these mysteries through all available means and the steadfast faith in a rational scientific approach to this task have thrust modern societies to the forefront of global development, and yielded enormous benefits for humans.

The Age of Enlightenment in Western thought began in 17th-century Europe, and spread to the American colonies, spurring a new enthusiasm for scientific inquiry and intellectual development. Proponents did not reject the fundamental moral principles embedded in their religious and cultural traditions, but expanded their view to incorporate a growing consciousness of the human capacity for understanding the wonders of the natural world, which had previously been considered the realm of the divine. The result was a great flowering of creative inspiration and discovery, which laid the groundwork for the advances that freed many of the world's people from the age-old cares of daily life. From running water and indoor plumbing, to electric power, and motorized transportation—the conveniences of modern existence have performed the miracle of adding hours to every day of human life, reducing the need to perform many of the burdensome repetitive tasks required for survival. With time on our hands and new power sources at our command, we have managed to bend the forces of nature to our will, and surpass the wildest imaginings of our ancestors in scientific knowledge and technological skill.

By contrast, most African societies have remained bound in a cycle of underdevelopment and under education, offering only a substandard quality of life for vast segments of the population. It has been justly suggested that one element retarding development in black African countries is the adherence to a passive view of man's role in the natural world, and reluctance to embrace modern approaches that have been adopted by technologically advanced cultures worldwide. A well-founded concern is that, lacking the will to harness nature's power, black Africans will remain at her mercy, and the harsh necessities of scraping an existence out of difficult environment with depleted resources will defeat all hope of claiming the better life that all Africa's people should enjoy.

The ability to adapt to changing environments extends beyond the immediate needs of pure survival in the material world; keeping abreast of technological advances can mean the difference between cultural survival and extinction, as it has for so many societies throughout human history. Black African nations are operating in a globally competitive environment— which requires rising to the challenge of global competition in all spheres of human endeavor. With the rich natural, mineral, and human resources that abound in black African countries, success is for the making, if Africans will make it so.

The stigma of poverty

The psychological effects of long-term deprivation can be devastating, and people who never enjoyed the benefits or comforts of modern life can be especially susceptible to related disruptions to their sense of self and their place in the world. There is a tendency for those afflicted to relinquish all aspirations for controlling the events that shape their lives, and to resign themselves to fate. At the other end of the scale are those who may develop an exaggerated sense of their worth that bears no connection to the reality of their situation. Either way, the mentality of the chronically poor can become an impediment to escaping from the poverty that afflicts them.

To break this cycle of poverty and despair, the people of black Africa must learn a new attitude toward the future—one that encompasses a wider range of possibilities and hold out the hope for real and lasting change. The effort to lift Africa's burden of underdevelopment must also offer strategies to break the ancient hold of superstition and mysticism on the people. African customs, beliefs and tools must undergo refinement that reflect continual human advancement and address changes in human needs. Time and energy will be required in abundance, but more importantly, the will to change things for the better.

CHAPTER 3

Superstition and Perceptions of the Natural World

"Failure to weigh our beliefs is a transgression against mankind. Society might if we believe in the wrong things or become habitually credulous."
Clifford, "Ethics of Belief."

All humans are driven by a powerful desire to understand why things happen, and in the absence of rational explanations, many will turn to traditional beliefs and superstitions that attribute the cause of events to supernatural forces. Superstitious beliefs do not occur in a vacuum; they are woven into the fabric of folk traditions that are passed down from generation to generation. Powerful cultural pressures may condition members of a society to perform certain rituals to prevent negative consequences, or avoid other behaviors in expectation of good fortune. But, most importantly, superstition can paralyze the minds of believers, forcing them to adopt an irrational mental attitude shaped by fear of the unknown.

Superstition and spirituality

Superstition may be viewed by some as related to spirituality and those who oppose both often consider them interchangeable, as though they share similar characteristics. However, since spirituality may involve a religious experience not driven by a morbid fear of the supernatural, it is possible to be spiritual and not superstitious—but it may be difficult to be superstitious and not spiritual. In any case, one aspect that the two belief systems clearly share is that they both resist the introduction of inquiry or verification. Of course there are many puzzling and unnerving phenomena that science and rational thought have yet to explain, but attributing natural occurrences to the direct intervention of a divine or supernatural agent creates an impermeable mental stronghold that resists reason and deters human progress.

Though some forms of superstitious belief exist and persist in all societies, in advanced modern cultures they generally remain within manageable bounds, and have little or no impact on human progress. By contrast, in black African societies, superstition has a crippling effect on the individual drive to explore, understand and create. Across Africa, a wide variety of superstitious beliefs have bound Africans to a world of fear and suspicion. The sight of an owl during the day is considered an evil omen; stumbling on the left foot portends bad luck, as does hitting a duck with a car; an itching left palm is believed to portend a loss of money, while an itching right palm heralds financial gain or a gift of cash. Imagine a world where profit or loss in business can be determined by which of a CEO's palm feels itchy on a particular day.

Victims of superstition — the most vulnerable members of society

Since superstition is not based on rational thought, but instead feeds on deep, primordial human fears, those who bear the brunt of its powerful destructive influence are often the least able to defend themselves in the social hierarchy. The elderly and sick, and women and children—especially those who are unprotected by strong family connections—may find themselves the victims of arbitrary and indiscriminate accusations, and suffer terrible punishments that are entirely undeserved.

It is a perplexing irony that in African societies that pride themselves on treating elders with reverence and respect, old people are frequently stigmatized as witches, and persecuted. The aged and infirm in many rural African communities are viewed either as witches or victims of witchcraft, which is widely believed to cause degenerative conditions associated with aging, such as Alzheimer's disease, hypertension, diabetes, hearing or memory loss, and the many symptoms of menopause.

Women are particularly susceptible to accusations of witchcraft, and may be tortured or murdered on suspicion of having caused harm through their supposed supernatural powers. This is especially true if they somehow fail in their role of child-bearing; in cases of infertility, childhood disease, or accidents causing the death of a child, the mother is often accused of causing the misfortune, and is persecuted by her spouse or social group.

Once again, it is a cruel irony that children may likewise suffer stigmatization due to superstitious beliefs that bear no relation to fact. The brutality of rejecting or discarding human children is shocking to the modern mind, but these practices have persisted to the present day in Sub-Saharan Africa. For example, it is believed in certain regions that albinos are a curse; likewise twin babies are seen as the sign of a curse on a family, and twins are therefore subject to abandonment or ostracism.

Anecdote #:1. A Child Abandoned to Die

A couple living in a village a few miles from the Atlantic coast gave birth to fraternal twins of mixed gender, and abandoned the children to die in the forest shortly after they were born. The parents were acting on the superstitious belief that such twins were a sign of evil, and would bring bad luck to the family.

Villagers who had been exposed to Christian sermons condemning such practices reported the incident to the local preacher, who rushed to the place where the babies had been abandoned—but when he arrived, the male child had already died. The preacher took the surviving infant home to his wife, who had just given birth to her own daughter, and she nursed both children. After the couple had cared for the baby for a few months, they offered her for adoption by a childless Christian friend (Justus Ogula. Personal communication).

Belief in witchcraft – paralyzing inquiry

The traditional rituals devised to "verify" claims against alleged witches and other suspected practitioners of black magic often involve dangerous and even fatal physical trials, and the life of the accused may depend on the outcome. They may be beaten until they confess, or required to drink noxious, hallucinogenic or poisonous concoctions. Other, less brutal, techniques involve divination by slaughtering animals and interpreting the remains—but of course none of these rites bear any connection with factual reality or empirical investigation. They either subject the accused to further abuse, or leave their fate in the hands of pure chance. Below is a report about a 4-year girl abused and persecuted for allegedly being a witch until local police in Nigeria rescued her.

Anecdote #: 2. A Child in a Cage

The Ondo State Police Commissioner, disclosed details to journalists that the police arrested the culprit, Mary Matthew, a woman who is a foster parent of the victim [the caged girl].

The Police Commissioner stated that Mrs. Matthew and her husband alleged that the young girl was possessed and that they needed to lock her outside of their apartment.

On receipt of the information, personnel attached to Juvenile Welfare Centre (JVC) visited the scene and met the girl in a cage as reported.

The young girl was immediately rescued and taken to the Police Clinic for proper medical attention. The girl narrated how she was severely abused in the care of her foster parents. She disclosed that all efforts to run away from her foster family failed because she was afraid of being killed. "This wicked woman [Mary] always tied me on my hands and forced me inside the cage while she flogged me with a horse whip every day," the little girl said.8

Perhaps it is natural that trials to determine unverifiable facts should consist of processes that serve no empirical function; after all, if supernatural events could be scientifically verified, they would not be considered supernatural in the first place. But as long as such abusive and illogical measures are employed in the name of beliefs, customs and social justice, no one in the community can ever feel safe from harm. At the word of a single accuser, anyone may be ostracized banished, beaten, burned, or murdered, with no recourse or claim to fair and impartial judgment. This is the definition of a prehistoric society.

How superstitions operate, propagate and become entrenched

Most humans do not subject their socially formed beliefs and habits to doubt or rigorous questioning; instead they tend to embrace the belief system operating within their society, and adopt the associated behaviors to find and strengthen their place within the group. This is a normal part of socialization, and the process is often unconscious, or only slightly regulated by purposeful decision making.

A common example can illustrate how we internalize social expectations is shaving: If shaving is the socially accepted norm, most people shave without questioning the reason for doing so. They embrace and justify the generally held belief that shaving is essential for proper grooming, and a few may rationalize the underlying principle that being clean-shaven is somehow more appropriate or even healthier than wearing a beard. Similarly, people who are raised in an environment in which wearing a beard is the social norm may develop their own personal justification for conforming to that behavior, or simply accept the habitual practice because "that's the way it has always been."

In black Africa, belief in superstition is the socially accepted norm; it influences human behavior in all spheres of life, including socially, politically, and economically. The enduring reliance on superstitious practice in African culture stems from the prevailing belief that all of life's challenges are caused by malevolent supernatural forces beyond human control. Even among the highly educated, many still succumb to the fears, anxieties, and mass hysterias induced by superstitious beliefs. Acquiescent behavior by the educated classes gives credence to fallacies that are rooted in irrational thought, and this reinforces bounded thinking among the general public. Conformance by prominent figures in society not only encourages the destructive practices associated with superstitious beliefs, but also stifles alternative lines of inquiry that could liberate the minds of all Africans and foster intellectual growth. This pathological cycle of adherence to age-old superstitions presents a formidable obstacle to the development of positive attitudes and behaviors that could improve the human condition throughout the African continent.

Superstition is a manifestation of the failure to distinguish between facts determined by evaluating verifiable evidence and beliefs based on social traditions untested by empirical means. It is completely irrational to believe that the mechanical operations of a factory could stall because someone cast a spell on the machines, or sprinkling holy water could prevent disease, or a high rate of car crashes at a dangerous bend on a highway could be caused by evil forces. The acceptance of such fantastical explanations reveals a deep underlying need for reassurance in the face of misfortune, and establishing a sense of human control over events that cause suffering and death. Ironically, superstition can prevent people from taking actions that could affect the outcome of some events, and thus increase the level of human control over the natural environment.

People whose lives are governed by superstition may impose cruel sanctions on those who they mistakenly identify as agents of evil forces, and communities driven by a system of superstitious belief accept the brutal punishments inflicted on these undeserving victims. This general acquiescence breeds a poisonous social climate that reinforces behaviors harmful to the victims themselves, as well as society overall. In some communities, those accused of supernatural evil deeds, are paraded in a public spectacle to shame them into confession, and crowds eagerly await the admission of diabolical acts committed by the alleged witch. Though victims of such persecution may express shock and confusion at the outrageous accusations, their reactions are interpreted as evidence of guilt. The heavy emotional toll levied on these victims, as well as their children and relatives, instills a feeling of personal vulnerability and lasting injury. People who endure this kind of persecution develop a weakened sense of control over their own lives, and are prone to psychological withdrawal. The social practices of cultures driven by superstitious beliefs thus engender an atmosphere of fear, anxiety, uncertainty, and ambiguity that weakens the chances for advancement of entire communities.

Social practices influenced by superstition have mired black Africans in a cycle of credulity and ignorance, unable to accept concrete explanations for the natural processes that drive their everyday lives. This imposes severe limitations on the ability of Africans to improve their own lives and the societies in which they participate, and restricts their capacity to amass the vital resources required to meet current and future challenges.

How superstition directly hinders development

Deeply embedded superstitious beliefs not only impede the intellectual growth of individuals and cultural enrichment of society, it also prevents development in more immediate and concrete ways. The lack of infrastructure in much of rural black Africa and structural inadequacies in many urban surroundings represent one of the most pressing problems affecting black Africans today, and superstitious beliefs can directly thwart development projects that would relieve this terrible burden.

Communities in thrall to age-old superstitions may spend more resources in appeasing the dead and "evil spirits" on infrastructural development than open roads to a real understanding of human connections with the forces of nature that may influence their lives. The result is a self-perpetuating cycle of ignorance and disenfranchisement that cripples generation after generation of black Africans, especially those living in rural communities.

Superstition feeds fear, suspicion, and paranoia

The enormous influence that superstition wields over the minds of ordinary black people makes them vulnerable to manipulation, exploitation, and abuse by unscrupulous people. One of the greatest dangers of superstition is that it encourages false attribution of causation that can nourish unfounded fears. For example, in the absence of routine medical autopsies to verify the cause of death, people often rely on the services of a witch doctor to investigate how and why their relatives died. In many cases, the verdict is that the death was caused by an envious family member, friend, or neighbor. In the eyes of a witch doctor, no one ever dies of old age, and death is hardly ever due to natural causes or diseases, as in diabetes, heart attack, AIDS, or cancer. Even automobile and motorcycle accidents and plane crashes are often attributed to evil spirits or witches.

Throughout black Africa, tales abound about people casting evil spells against their enemies on employment, promotion, and other human conditions. Witches are accused of causing financial hardship, and illness - AIDS, cancer, diabetes, infertility, and death. While rational-minded people may find these ideas absurd, those who believe wholeheartedly in these kinds of malevolent supernatural powers may visit terrible retribution on those they suspect of possessing it. Within this new millennium, numerous alleged penis snatchers have been lynched by angry mobs.

In "A Mind Dismembered. In Search of the Magical Penis Thieves," journalist Frank Bures describes perennial hysteria surrounding tales of male genitalia disappearance as a "culture-bound syndrome," or type of mental affliction that arises directly out of a particular sociocultural milieu. He relates his own attempt to enter the mindset that could produce this seemingly fantastical belief, and his appreciation for the real fear felt by the "victim" of a so-called penis snatcher. He concludes: "Every culture has its own logic, its own beliefs, its own stresses. Once one buys into its assumptions, one becomes a prisoner to the logic. For some people, that means a march toward its more tragic conclusions."[9] To end the tragic march toward a future without hope of advancement, it will be necessary to alter the dysfunctional belief systems that can create such powerful, dangerous, and irrational fears in otherwise normal, healthy human beings.

Superstition closes the door to reason and critical thinking, and believers are left ignorant and vulnerable to the destructive forces of nature and cultural prejudice. This effect is particularly evident in problem-plagued black Africa, where ancestral practices collide with Christian and Islamic religious beliefs, and all of these traditions compete in offering their own spiritual solutions to natural problems.

Alignment of traditional beliefs with imported religion in black Africa

Few would argue that religion plays a significant role in the human experience. It fulfills human aspirations for affiliation, fellowship, sanctification, and connection with the supernatural. However, credulous acceptance of any form of religious belief creates a distorted view of reality harmful to individuals and society as a whole. Thus Christian religion with, its tranquilizing sermons, imprisons the mind and, as a result, has left millions of black Africans at the margins of progress and development.[10]

In many African countries, evangelical religion is growing at an accelerated pace. But in light of the serious developmental challenges facing Africa, the influence of contemporary religion on poverty must be thoroughly examined. Two areas of concern that need to be addressed are: (1) the emergence of the theology of affluence in Africa, and (2) teachings that propagate or reinforce belief in witchcraft that creates fear and credulous followership.[11]

It is evident that African Christians are increasingly embracing the theology of affluence, but this has translated neither to an acceptance of the theology of liberation, nor collective African prosperity. Instead, the new found theology of affluence is closely wedded to the corrupt social, economic, and political systems found in most black African countries. Leaders of these churches use their congregations as platforms for easy access to wealth, power, and influence. Consequently, while the pastors or leaders live in affluence, the teeming majority live in abject poverty. Blinded by faith and lacking the capability to interrogate their leaders and their own beliefs, the poor flock into these religious organizations, sacrificing their meager finances to the organization and its leaders. For the majority, the church is a means of escaping the pain and suffering caused by excruciating poverty.[12]

The contagion of relying on providence has no boundaries; it has spread among middle class hard working Africans at home and abroad. Believers have been seduced into these churches in the hope of improving their financial status and lives. Members believe that by divine intervention their debts and financial burdens will be eliminated.[13]

In the summer of 2013, as part of the ritual of invoking the Holy Spirit, an African Pastor in Brooklyn, New York, USA, asked members to present before God their wallets, purses, bills and, other symbols associated with money for sanctification either for a bounty of cash, or to eliminate unpaid bills, loans, and other debts. While there may be no shortage of arguments to support prosperity teachings, their impact on people's financial health can hardly be measured. Merely relying on prosperity sermons without engaging in productive work is most likely to lead ardent believers on a path to financial ruin. Whether or not prosperity is the motivation for attending these churches, believers ought to examine their transactional approach to building a relationship with God.[14]

The second concern is about the teachings or influence of contemporary Pentecostal religion that reinforces beliefs in witchcraft.

The most pervasive of such teachings is the dangerous cocktail of traditional beliefs in witches and mysticism with references to demons and evil spirits in the Bible. Beliefs in witches and magic have influenced African phenomenology for centuries. However, reinforcing these beliefs with Christian doctrines is an added obstacle to liberating the African mind. Sermons that strengthen beliefs in witches and evil spirits exploit the human tendency to be afraid of the unknown. Church leaders orchestrate these fears with portents of doom and gloom, creating an atmosphere of mutual suspicion and division in families. Consequently, believers become afraid of their husbands, wives, parents, children, siblings and relatives, believed to have sinister plots to harm them. Pastors who propagate these beliefs hold church members in psychological bondage while cashing in financially.[15]

The extent to which this perverted brand of Christianity has captured the minds of Africans is illustrated in the widely publicized YouTube video of Bishop David Oyedepo, a Nigerian church leader, is seen slapping a female church member accused of being a witch.[16] Outraged, a viewer who saw the video commented: "Who's worse off, Oyedepo or the fools cheering for the fear mongering idiot?"[17] Many found it disturbing that, in the name of God, members of the congregation continued to support and applaud Bishop Oyedepo, even when his theatrics degenerated to a physical assault on the girl. In a more shocking case, a pastor doused a member of his congregation in gasoline and set the person ablaze.

Combatting superstition in black African communities

Societies that have found ways to manage their affairs have also found ways to overcome the incapacitating influence of superstitious beliefs. But where a majority of the population believes that witchcraft and other evil forces act directly in their daily lives, it is difficult to convince them of concrete reality. This makes the task of liberating the minds of black Africans from the influence of superstition especially daunting. Nevertheless, the burden of ignorance that superstition has placed on many Africans must be eliminated if development is to go forward on the continent. This will require a revolution in thought and behavior that can only be achieved through retrospective reflection and education, leading to a fundamental transformation in some aspects of African tradition.

The mindset that attributes all natural events to supernatural forces must be changed to one that is lodged in the process of factual discovery. As Africans develop their capacity for inquiry and exploration, they will gain a new understanding of their environment, and build a coherent system of responses to the problems afflicting their societies. For example, progress in healthcare can only be made by addressing the tragic misunderstanding that attributes AIDS, Alzheimer's disease, symptoms of menopause, cancer and other diseases to witchcraft or evil spirits. Black Africans must strive to overcome the limitations imposed by their cultural conditioning and belief in superstition and to embrace the scientific methods of observation, fact-gathering, and experimentation.

Africa needs a cultural reformation similar to the revolution in thought and belief that transformed Western societies during the 17th and 18th centuries and liberated the minds of Europeans from the shackles of superstitious thought. Before the scientific awakening ushered in by the era of Isaac Newton;[18] most people explained the workings of the world around them in terms of supernatural forces and divine influence. If an individual sustained an injury, crops failed, or any other natural disaster struck mankind, the event was attributed to God's will. These perceptions gradually changed as scientific explanations of natural events came to light through discovery and invention. Rational minds began to espouse the view that God had established a universe based on certain principles, and that human beings have a right - even a duty - to explore and understand how it functions. This was a historical turning point at which humanity began a concentrated search for the fundamental laws that govern nature. Instead of blindly resigning themselves to fate, people began to focus on developing the capacity to improve their own lives through inquiry, discovery, and technological advancement.

Since superstitious traditions and practices have been embedded in African culture for millennia, the problem will not be solved without assistance from educated Africans at home and in the diaspora, who can bring new perspectives to bear, and provide important insights as well as organizational support.

Progressive education is the key that can unlock the door to a wider world of scientific knowledge and technological understanding, and prepare the coming generations of black Africans for participation in modern society. By casting off the dark shadow of ancient fears that have stifled progress and sowed dissension among families and communities throughout the Sub-Saharan region, African nations can bring on the dawn of a new "age of enlightenment" that is all their own.

CHAPTER 4

Education and Illiteracy in Black Africa

"A child miseducated is a child lost"
John F. Kennedy.

One of the greatest burdens afflicting black African societies today is the high rate of illiteracy in comparison with other populations worldwide. In 2015, more than 25 percent of the world's illiterate adults lived in the Sub-Saharan region,[19] which is home to about 12 percent of the world's people.

> Adult literacy rates were below 50% in the following 14 countries: Afghanistan, Benin, Burkina Faso, Central African Republic, Chad, Côte d'Ivoire, Ethiopia, Guinea, Haiti, Liberia, Mali, Mauritania, Niger, Senegal, Sierra Leone and South Sudan. Youth literacy rates, for the population aged 15 to 24 years, are generally higher than adult literacy rates, reflecting increased access to schooling among younger generations.[20]

The ability to read and write a native language is taken for granted among citizens of developed countries, where high standards of education and near-universal primary and secondary school attendance are the rules. In most of black Africa, insufficient early schooling, with a gender bias disfavoring education for girls, has left millions of individuals unable to participate in any of the crucial daily activities that depend on basic literacy. This "functional disability" has profound effect on psychological health as well as personal, social, and cultural development, and thus impedes national progress in every field of human endeavor.

The world's lowest literacy rates are found in Senegal, Mali, Niger, Chad, and Ethiopia, where less than 50 percent of the adult population can read and write.[21] In order to break the cycle of illiteracy and ignorance that has continued to plague the continent, the multifaceted problem of language standardization and education must be tackled not only at the grass-roots level, but on a national scale.

The 2010 UNESCO "Education for All Global Monitoring Report" indicates that "about 38 percent of the adult population in Sub-Saharan Africa or 153 million adults, lack the basic literacy and numeracy skills needed in everyday life."[22] This is a staggering figure, especially given the widespread underdevelopment, economic stagnation, chronic poverty, insufficient health care, frequent conflict, perennial famine, and poor infrastructure that characterize so much of black Africa. Can the problem of illiteracy be adequately addressed, while so many other urgent concerns require immediate attention? Lacking the basics of daily sustenance, why should families prioritize schooling over finding enough to eat, or clean water to drink? Yet, throughout the continent, poor, illiterate people struggle to send their children to school, in the hope of providing a better future for them. It is a heroic effort in the face of nearly insurmountable odds.

Education and literacy hold the keys to all modern human development, and the skills and knowledge students gain from primary school through university offer not only the hope of personal and professional advancement, but also a brighter outlook for the communities in which they live and work. It is the students of today who will build the world of tomorrow, and if black Africa is to prosper in the years to come, concerted effort must be made to lift the heavy burden of epidemic illiteracy that afflicts its people today.

Those who lack reading and writing skills are severely disadvantaged in a world that increasingly relies on written communication. Every aspect of modern life requires basic literacy—from deciphering simple signs and labels to understanding directions, instructions, safety alerts, and other warnings. It goes without saying that proficient literacy is a prerequisite for access to promising jobs, comprehensive healthcare, and the realms of commerce and finance. Emphasizing the importance of literacy in employment, George Agyros, (Personal communication), the human resources manager in a mid-sized New York City agency noted that if an educated worker and an uneducated worker are assigned similar tasks, the educated worker will perform the duties more efficiently than the uneducated worker who learned the procedures by rote.

Given the fundamental role that written language plays in our lives, and the profound negative impact on quality of life that results when basic literacy is not guaranteed through universal access to early education, it seems fitting that this access is included in Article 26 of the United Nations' Universal Declaration of Human Rights:

> Everyone has the right to education. Education shall be free, at least in the elementary and fundamental stages. Elementary education shall be compulsory. Technical and professional education shall be made generally available and higher education shall be equally accessible to all on the basis of merit.[23]

Long roots of illiteracy – the legacy of unwritten language

One aspect of the black African literacy dilemma derives from the history of indigenous African cultures that have been based on oral tradition. Though the linguistic diversity of the Sub-Saharan region is unparalleled, there is no corresponding wealth of textually-based culture.[24] As a result, the pronounced cultural norms still favor oral over written communication. Most African tribes did not develop their native languages into a written form that entered general use, let alone served as the foundation of a cultural or historical record. Therefore, almost all written communication now takes place in the native tongues of European ex-colonists, which have become the official language in most African countries.

Since formal education in black Africa is conducted in ex-colonial languages, it carries a psychological baggage related to the history of domination by conquering powers, and subjugation to their will. In order to become well-educated, black Africans must submit to a form of cultural oppression that has long outlasted the end of European colonialism, and will doubtless continue to operate for the foreseeable future. The problem of an indigenous instructional language for education and administration will remain in the absence of standardized languages within regions.

Ex-colonial languages are still maintained in most black African countries as the official language to avoid conflict among competing ethnic groups, though the use of native languages in formal education has its proponents. *Aboki 4 Christ*, a Nigerian comedian describes his excruciating ordeal learning English as a foreign language in a comic script. The full translation of Aboki's script is provided below.

The fact that I'm able to speak English before you is a miracle worthy of giving testimony. I Aboki, making you laugh with my jokes in English …let me praise God.

I actually grew up in the northern part of Nigeria where everything in my school, everything we were taught was delivered in the Hausa language, including English — English language classes were taught in Hausa. For example, if my teacher says; "this is a ball," we moped confused, until she says, "na go dey...." [Thank you] Then we all respond in Hausa saying "yowu wah madam" [Affirming].

It was such that Hausa was spoken both inside and outside the class. Then one day, the Commissioner for Education visited my school. As soon as he came into my class, we stood up and greeted him "Sanu dey zuwa oga" in the Hausa language [meaning "Welcome Commissioner!]. This was seen an abomination or a disgrace to the school. The Commissioner, displeased by the use of vernacular in our greeting and asked our teacher. "Madam what kind of children are you preparing for me in this school?" He banned vernacular speaking in the school, imposing a penalty of 24 strokes of the cane for any child who violated the rule.

"People of God," Aboki exclaimed, and continued, from that day children who were unable to express themselves in English, became "deaf and dumb" in the classroom. If a child wanted to borrow a pencil from a classmate, the child would concoct some gibberish, "go beh, eh be beh," along with gestures. "Amen!" [The audience roared with laughter] — That basically was the mode of communication until one day I felt pressed while my teacher was teaching. I needed to ease myself, but didn't know how I could express that to my teacher in English. English then was an insurmountable hurdle to overcome. When my teacher turned to write on the board, I attempted to sneak out of the classroom, but my teacher turned around just as I took my first step and said: "Yes, Aboki, why are you standing? What is your problem?" Since I could not express myself in English, I could only say, "madam, problem, problem, ah ah eh, eh …" (gesturing and wriggling). Unable to say anything meaningful, I sat down.

After a while, the pressure became unbearable so I stood up again. My teacher asked why I was standing… This time I responded; "madam, madam, water body tweeeh.. eh." "What is the meaning of that? "Will you sit down, my friend?" my teacher retorted, and I sank back into my chair.

But God seemed to be on my side, my teacher's phone started ringing. As she left the class to receive her call, I thanked God and started for the other door. As fortune would have it, I mistakenly stepped on the toe of a female classmate, "Vero," She was one of those spoiled brats we called "ajeboh" [children raised with butter or privileged children]. Just as I stepped on her toe, she landed a slap across my check. It hurt so bad, the urge to ease myself almost ceased. But remember, we were banned from expressing ourselves in vernacular. So I could only point at her grouching "ah, ah, Vero, ah, ah, Vero ah." Then she unleashed English on me asking, "where were you going to? Because madam is not in the class, you were running around; you stepped on my toe, and I slapped you." "Um tuuh!" [It serves you right]. Still, I could only mutter "eh eh (pointing and crying) 'Vero' ..." As I was struggling to come up with words, the teacher returned to the classroom. She asked what was happening. The girl explained saying, "I do not know where he was going to. Because you went out of the class, he was running around, and he stepped on my toe, so I slapped him." The teach turned to me as asked me for my version of what happened, which of course exacerbated my ordeal

I said: "Madam, eh eh, (pointing) madam, eh eh, madam" "What was the problem Aboki?" the teacher repeated. I said, "madam Oh O Oh .... " The teacher then said "Aboki if you cannot say what happened, you should sit down." I tried again to utter some words "madam, it's me o, is me he sit down, is me he won do 'tur-ruh' [I wanted to go and urinate]. The teacher, getting exasperated, said: "What do you mean?" I said madam "is me he stand; is me is walk; is me nor see; is march [step] is Vero, is 'kpoweie,' [sound of a slap on the check] madam, whaai?"

Realizing Aboki could not express himself in English, the teacher said: "Aboki you are a disgrace; does it mean you can't tell me what happened between the two of you in simple English?" "In fact Aboki, I want you to make a sentence with the word 'yam.' "Yam?" I repeated, then said, "Madam I chop [eat] yam." My teacher said, "No, not good enough; I want you to make a longer sentence." "A longer sentence? Ok madam," "I chop [eat] yam Ohoooooo... it is longer."

Infuriated, my teacher assigned me home work to be prepared to make three good English sentences the following day and that if I failed, I was going to be demoted from primary 4 to 2. Only three sentences, I thought "madam, nor wor-ries, I will do that tomorrow. I decided that I will start by picking up English sentences from anyone I hear speaking English and regurgitate them the next day.

First, on my way home, I heard some students fighting, and one of them said. "What's wrong with you? Are you sure you are okay?" Are you sure you are okay? I repeated, that sounds very good. I kept repeating the sentence as I walked home. In fact, anyone that said hello to me on my way received the response "Yes, are you sure you are okay?" Then as I got closer to home, I saw a man and a woman quarreling — The woman was saying "I'm not going to take this non-sense, I'm not going to take it. What kind of a thing is this?" To which the man responded: "Stop barking like a dog?" Stop barking like a dog" I repeated the sen-tence. I got my second sentence.

Finally, when I got to my compound, a family was preparing to go out, but their daughter, "Judith" was delaying and her mother was urging her to hurry up, while the father said: "Come on baby, let's go." "Come on baby, let's go;" my three sentences were complete.

When I got to school the next day, my teacher seems to have forgotten she gave me home work. Equipped with my three sentences, I started seeking attention. I wondered why my teacher is acting as though she never gave me an assignment now that I have learned to speak English. Why would she not invite so I could show off my English speaking ability to my classmates? I made every effort, standing up, pointing, even attempting to walk to the front of the classroom, to get my teacher's attention. She eventually noticed me and said: "Yes Aboki, come here! Yesterday, I said you must learn three English sentences. I want you to tell me the sentences you learned. I couldn't wait for her to finish before I started my first sentence. I said, "madam are you sure you are okay?" The teacher became upset and said "what kind of nonsense is that? Do you realize that ... Again, before she could finish her sentence, I said "madam, stop barking like a dog!' She became even more incensed saying, "Aboki you are calling me a dog?" I must make sure you're expelled from this school today. In fact, I'm taking you to the headmaster's office." Then I dropped my last sentence, "come on baby, let's go." [Audience roars with applause as the show ends].[25]

Aboki's experience, though a comic rendition, reflects the experience of countless children struggling to express themselves in a foreign language; petrified by the experience early in life, many African children never overcome the fear of their lack of proficiency in English or French and are unable to advance their abilities.

While several African languages Hausa, Swahili, Zulu, Ibo, Yoruba, and Ijaw, are spoken by millions, few expect they will gain global prominence in the near future. Therefore, black Africans seeking education that will allow them to fulfill ambitions beyond their national borders will value fluency in the languages that will grant them access to a wider range of opportunities. Furthermore, languages, such as English and French, are globally dominant in the halls of political and economic power, and even citizens of smaller European countries must become fluent in one of these more widely-used tongues if they want to participate as equals on an international stage.

The cultural and technological benefits that a mastery of foreign languages offers to black Africans are highly valued, and the ability to record and share information has been widely appreciated and embraced

since colonial times. Colonial languages remain the standard in education and government, newspaper and book publication, and international commerce. However, the societal transformation to a culture of
literacy is complex, as some Sub-Saharan nations are still struggling to
meet the millennial development goals on literacy.

The shame of illiteracy – a personal burden

In a world increasingly driven by textual communication through
countless media, children and adults who get a late start or who never
achieve basic literacy may suffer a sense of inadequacy and personal failure. This is even more true in technologically disadvantaged black Africa,
where the lack of resources and opportunities renders interpersonal competition all the more acute. Since every hope of advancement hangs on
the ability to read and write in English or French, those who lack this
ability, or who speak only a native language, may be limited to a life of
subservient work in low-level positions, or manual labor in agriculture
or manufacturing. It is not an outlook that encourages pride and self-
confidence, or a sense of security in the world.

The millions of black Africans who are unable to read and write
remain dependent on others for basic everyday communications and
tasks; adults may have to rely on their school-age children to decode simple instructions, or on the help of friends and neighbors to transcribe or
transmit private messages. The reliance on others to read, interpret, and
write can be a matter of privacy, pride, or humiliation. This kind of
chronic humiliation can create an indelible sense of social inferiority
that stifles or warps ambition, and breeds bitter disaffection. Because
illiteracy is so widespread, the cumulative toll on social coherence and
functionality is enormous.

In April, 2016, the *Vanguard*, a Nigerian newspaper, published the
story about a 60 year old man, Adelabu, attending secondary school in
the Niger Delta region of Nigeria. He was motivated by the desire to
overcome what he described is the perpetual pain of being illiterate in a
modern world where everything was driven by one's ability to read and
write in English. [26] According to the report Adelabu's mother died when
he was a child and he had to live with several relatives; the dislocation
and lack of support forced him to drop out of school. As a result, he did

menial jobs from childhood to support himself. Adelabu believes that a secondary school education will free him from depending on others to read, interpret or write for him for the rest of his life.

The rift between the literate and illiterate is comparable to the rich and poor, or are closely associated, since access to education is tied to material wealth. Because knowledge truly is power in any society, those who are deprived of education due to poverty are doubly disadvantaged, and doubly stigmatized. More tragically still, they are caught in a destructive cycle that is almost impossible to escape.

Anecdote #: 3. A Matter of Privacy

A woman living in a remote village wanted to relay a message discreetly to her son who lived in the city. She was informed by a close friend that of a plot by members of her extended family to sell a piece land that had been allotted to her son. However, she could neither read nor write, and had never been to the city herself.

The woman learned that an acquaintance in the village was about to travel to the city, and could deliver a written message to her son. She then did what most illiterate Africans in her situation would do—she sought someone who could read and write, to help her compose a letter. She reached out to a local teacher, who transcribed her message, read it aloud to her, put it in an envelope, and sealed it. Though the privacy of her communication seemed secure, she had already put its confidentiality at risk.

She gave the letter to her acquaintance, who traveled to the city and delivered it to her son. Upon receipt of the letter, her son rushed home and foiled the plot to sell his land. The woman was pleased with the result of her intervention—but her triumph was short-lived. Word of her actions had leaked out to the conspirators through the only source that had knowledge of her letter—the person who had helped her to write it. As a result, she was ostracized by the angry family members who would have gained financially from the sale of the land.

Gender and literacy – society suffers when women can't read and write

Female literacy is one of the most significant factors influencing life expectancy during childbirth in developing countries. Women who can read and write, and had access to basic education tend to bear fewer children and live longer than women without basic education, who bear many children with higher mortality rate. [27] Literate women are also better at managing household finances, and contribute more to family income through self-employment, small business ownership, or employment. Unfortunately, gender disparities in Sub-Saharan Africa result in lower rates of school attendance for girls, and societal pressure for women to remain exclusively in a maternal or caregiving role.

Despite some modest gains in primary education for girls, gender differences in literacy stubbornly persist. UNESCO regional overview of Sub-Saharan Africa in 2011 described the problem of gender disparities in the region:

> Gender disparities in adult literacy are still very marked in Sub-Saharan Africa. On average, literacy rates for women were three-quarters the level of those for men in 2008. In fourteen countries, they were less than two-thirds as high. Patterns of literacy are also strongly related to wealth and household location. In Burundi, about two-thirds of women in the wealthiest 20% of households are literate, compared with less than one-fifth in the poorest 20% of households, and women living in urban areas are more likely to be literate than women living in rural areas.[28]

Since few gains are being seen in secondary education for girls, the outlook for wide-scale empowerment and emancipation of black African women seems bleak.[29] Nevertheless, some women whose own prospects are limited by poverty and illiteracy become passionate advocates of education for their children, and make enormous sacrifices to ensure that they remain in school. Without concerted public and private efforts at the local, state, and national levels, future generations of women and children are at risk of continuing the cycle of ignorance and disadvantage.

The right to literacy

The development of written language has allowed human societies to record their history or culture for posterity, communicate at a distance, and relate narratives from individual perspectives. Lacking this capacity, individuals and communities can have only limited ability to generalize knowledge or transfer information beyond their immediate environment. In the words of former US President William Clinton, on the occasion of International Literacy Day in 1994, "Literacy is not a luxury; it is a right and a responsibility. And in an international community increasingly dedicated to the principles of equality and opportunity, illiteracy is unacceptable."[30]

Literacy offers freedom of interaction among geographically dispersed individuals and groups, and illiteracy denies people this freedom. In all, the ability to read and write language has come to represent an integral part of the human cultural construct to the extent that in most societies today, it is an indispensable tool for survival, and for individual and social development.

Literacy encompasses the ability to read, write, basic numeracy skills, and apply these skills constructively and creatively. A majority of black Africans are deficient in the ability to read and write, which has an impact on Africa's prospects for advancement. The absence of an educated workforce in a modern competitive world exacerbates the problem of underdevelopment in black Africa.

The inability to read and write also has a direct impact on the rise of undemocratic governments in Africa in much of the post-independence era. An illiterate population is susceptible to manipulation by politicians and is generally responsible for the lack of accountability and good governance. Good education empowers individuals to pursue their dreams and reach their God given potential. Without generalized commercial, technical, and professional acumen and experience, it has been impossible to provide vast areas of the Sub-Saharan region with clean water, hygienic living conditions, and a safe environment in which to conduct normal social activities. In the chaotic, dysfunctional underdeveloped atmosphere that results, unstable and undemocratic governments have chronically failed to enact and enforce effective laws and regulations to protect individuals, businesses and property. How many of these problems could be resolved simply by ensuring that all black African children receive free, basic education, with support and encouragement to continue their studies and pursue productive careers?

Functional illiteracy – an equally destructive force

An assessment of the impact of illiteracy on black African progress must include reference to the large number of semi-illiterates on the continent. Increased access to schooling during the last half century has resulted in a corresponding increase in the number of functionally illiterate black

Africans. These are people who possess basic reading and writing skills, but are unable to process and assimilate basic written information, or complete related tasks. Some functional illiterates are hindered from making common daily decisions due to inadequate training in the application of knowledge and skills, or lack of appropriate social conditioning. These functional illiterates cannot fully comprehend signage, directions, and instructions they encounter daily, and instead they must almost entirely rely on word-of-mouth communication.

Anyone who travels by air is familiar with the myriad signs that are carefully placed to facilitate passengers' navigation through airport terminals. But in spite of these ubiquitous pointers, in large airports where the majority of passengers are black Africans, the boarding process often involves an overwhelming degree of chaos and confusion. Because so many of the travelers are fully or functionally illiterate, progress through the terminal and boarding procedures can slow to a crawl as people frantically seek simple information required to board the appropriate plane. In the worst-case scenario, most of the passengers ignore the pre-boarding instructions and surge forward at the gate, forcing airport officials to adopt strict and often demeaning control measures in some international terminals.

Functional illiteracy is a pernicious problem worldwide, and even in the most highly developed countries, it can represent a drag on productivity and cultural advancement that is very difficult to quantify or assess. But in black Africa, where the number of fully illiterate people and the level of general underdevelopment are both so high, this problem has a stronger impact, and requires more urgent action. Basic reading and writing skills must be enhanced by further development of the cognitive abilities required for processing the reading materials that all adults encounter daily. Lacking this fundamental investment in human capital, it will be difficult to achieve any of the other long-term goals for the development of black African nations.

"Functional illiteracy" – a waste of costly investment and priceless human potential

While the main literacy challenge in black Africa is represented by the complete illiteracy of people who can neither read nor write, and the functional illiteracy of those who cannot process written communication beyond the most basic level, there is another level of "illiteracy" that defies common sense and seems impervious to intervention. From a developmental perspective, this is perhaps the most devastating form of the illiteracy that has ravaged black Africa, because it represents a terrible waste of human investment, as well as the creative potential of Africans, which are the continent's best hope for cultural salvation.

The term "educated illiterate" is an oxymoron - as these two words have opposite meanings—and this emphasizes the irony of the phenomenon. Those who receive the benefit or gift of formal education should naturally be able to contribute the fruits of their learning to the society in which they live, and thus increase its level of cultural, technological, and commercial development. The knowledge and skills they receive should prepare them to function effectively as upstanding members of their community, or to work productively in any area of expertise they have chosen. Education prepares people to become productive members of society; hence education in black Africa should be designed with special reference to productivity. In an environment where capacity resources are scarce, education should never be wasted, and the benefits it provides should preferably be returned to the society that bestowed it.

Fulfilling the creative cycle of education, productive work, social and cultural development, and transfer of knowledge to the next generation requires a functioning engine of economic benefit, without which it is impossible to maintain a healthy society. Unfortunately, there is no such economic livewire functioning in black Africa, where a lack of investment in infrastructure and social development has left even wealthy, resource-rich nations mired in widespread poverty with all the scars it brings.

In many countries, as the educational standards collapse, instead of concentrating on their studies to achieve success, students rely on short-term rote learning to pass exams, or resort to cheating or bribing teachers who can barely subsist on their own wages. If the system devalues educational achievement, there is little sense of moral responsibility or personal pride of accomplishment attached to learning; intellectual development may also erode. Thus a student may pass through secondary school and even college or graduate school without developing critical reasoning, or learning how to apply knowledge effectively under changing circumstances. This is exactly the definition of "educated illiteracy."

Furthermore, because prominent positions may be awarded on the basis of family connections with wealth or political influence, there is little incentive for those who are not born to privilege to seek to advance their skills through education. This means that those who strive to achieve professional success may not be able to find employment commensurate with their skill level. The result can be a generalized sense of disillusionment with the whole concept of education and professional training.

A culture of intellectual apathy breeds illiteracy

Many Africans have demonstrated that they value education and, over the years, Africans have earned outstanding educational achievements in various fields; yet there remains an undercurrent of suspicion and apathy toward Western education. This feeling is bolstered by the notion that Western education alienates Africans from their culture and heritage. The view is most prevalent in underserved black communities worldwide.

In these communities there is seeming apathy toward education. Students who seek education as a means of elevating themselves out of poverty are often viewed as having "colonial mentality," or being "brainwashed," "sell-outs," or "acting white" by peers. But without education economic advancement becomes more challenging. Unless the social stigma is removed, the pursuit of personal advancement through intellectual development cannot be accomplished and the hope of achieving a more elevated status among the peoples of the world will remain elusive. Instead these Africans will have to resign to doing menial jobs like dragging garbage receptacles through airports and hallways of Western corporations, mopping bathroom floors, or cooking and serving meals - if they do not embrace the opportunities offered by education. Education viewed purely through the lens of assimilating other cultures, ideas, or education devoid of critical thinking and application is dangerous and must be discouraged. But education that develops an individual's capacity to think critically, that facilitates inquiry, discovery, and develops intellectual ability to evaluate phenomena is fundamental to human advancement. Application of the universal principles of education has far greater benefits to black Africans than reliance on knowledge of the past handed down orally from generation to generation.

CHAPTER 5

The Leadership Albatross

"Leadership is the capacity to translate vision into reality."
Warren G. Bennis.

Black Africa has produced a few notable visionary and heroic leaders, but the task of reforming corrupt, inefficient or oppressive governments and civil codes to conform with modern democratic practices has proven too challenging for most black African leaders -with only a few exceptions. Though many blame their failures on historical disadvantages, the appalling lack of progress can also be attributed, in large part, to flawed concepts of leadership, abuse of power, and self-defeating attitudes among the citizenry of post-colonial Sub-Saharan Africa. Accustomed to the abuses of exploitive and despotic leaders at every level of society, most ordinary black Africans can scarcely imagine what true democracy is, let alone demand its establishment, or lay its foundations. As long as bad leaders go unchallenged, coercive forms of leadership will continue to permeate all facets of black African life.

Since black Africans have collectively failed to construct functional social systems with well-defined roles for those charged with maintaining the wellbeing of the people, many leaders usurp or abuse the power they are granted or acquire. The vast majority of citizens unwittingly cede their civil rights to these despots because they are ignorant of the rights they have and are uneducated about the rights they could achieve in a more democratic society. Some are seduced by the personality and charisma of leaders who shower them with false

48

promises. Overwhelmed by years of suffering, others have simply resigned to their disempowerment, hoping a spiritual messiah will one day arise to save them. Meanwhile, these passive followers dutifully obey the commands of their leaders, in fear of ruthless reprisals should they show any sign of rebellion. Those who have achieved some level of personal comfort within oppressive social structures may show allegiance to despotic leaders while they are in power, and then attempt to fix blame on them after they have left office.

While developed and developing nations around the world have moved toward less autocratic models of government and leadership, most post-colonial African countries are still under dictatorial regimes based on primal notions of power and cults of personality. This destructive political climate has deepened black Africa's failure to progress in step with nations that have embraced modernity, and the opportunities it provides, for improving quality of life through technological and cultural advancement.

Since decolonization, ineffective and abusive leadership has been one of heaviest burdens stifling development throughout the Sub-Saharan region. The urgent leadership challenge is to foster good governance by developing strong democratic structures that can withstand the pressures of regressive factors, nepotism and corruption. Without strong, responsive, and dedicated leaders, it is hard to build functional governments that can ensure good education, infrastructural development, personal and national security, and a higher quality of life for all citizens.

Flawed leadership values – roadmaps for tyranny and chaos

A majority of Africans in leadership positions perceive their role as a "rulership," or unlimited exercise of the power derived from their office or official positions. This flawed perception enables the use of official power as a tool of oppression and government as a means of centralizing power, rather than as a reciprocal process between the leaders and the led.[31] Unfortunately, this attitude is deeply embedded in black African political culture, to the extent that if a man is pulled from the depths of the African forest to occupy any position of power, no matter the size of the entity, chances are he will quickly transform himself into a despot. As soon as the position is secured, the person manages the office as though they have been granted a license to convert public funds for personal use.

> **Anecdote # 4: The Tyrannical Headmaster**
>
> Mr. Didier was appointed headmaster of an elementary school in a remote village in West Africa, and his new found sense of authority in the community drew legitimacy from his elevated position. However, Didier never restrained himself from exercising his official power in order to gain compliance from teachers, students and even other members of the community. He established a small fiefdom where he ruled with an iron fist, and made decisions unilaterally. He was unfriendly and unapproachable, and tolerated no dissent.
>
> Though Didier had little more than a secondary school education, he acted as though he was the most intelligent and powerful man alive. On a few occasions, he locked the entire school population out of the building because the students and teachers had failed to obey his commands. Didier was dreaded by the other community members, who regularly offered him gifts in the form of farm produce, liquor, and gifts of money to ensure that their children remained in school.
>
> Didier ultimately became the sole authority in the locality, and unopposed by those who were lower in social rank, he felt responsible to no one. The teachers obeyed him obsequiously as though he was a supreme ruler, and his wives and children received the same deferential treatment that he was accorded. His iron-clad reign ended only after he was transferred to another school.

Didier's case illustrates how African individuals in positions of authority come to see themselves as the source of the power they have been granted or acquired. Such leaders can completely subjugate the people under their authority, who are often barely educated and lack the ability to resist these excesses.

Another common feature in the African leadership landscape is the "president-for-life" syndrome. A majority of the heads of state who assumed office in early post-colonial Africa attempted to hold onto power in perpetuity, establishing repressive regimes and instituting governance structures that would guarantee their longevity in office. Mobutu Sese Seko of Zaire, Muammar Gaddafi of Libya, Hosni Mubarak of Egypt, Ben Ali of Tunisia, Robert Mugabe of Zambia, Hastings Kamuzu Banda, Amadou Toumani Touré of Mali, and Yahya Jammeh, of Gambia are among the African leaders who ruled their countries for longer than two decades.

The bar has been set so low that when former Nigerian President Goodluck Jonathan conceded defeat in Nigeria's 2015 presidential election, he was hailed a hero for doing what is taken for granted in a normal democracy. The reason for hailing Jonathan is understandable. Many African leaders assume office, promising democracy only to become consumed by the allure of power and aim to keep it at all cost - i.e. Mugabe of Zimbabwe and Yoweri Museveni of Uganda.

Museveni was a vocal critic of African leaders who held on to power. He even seduced Western governments for instituting economic and political reforms. But nearly three decades later, Museveni is still in power, and his demeanor increasingly resembles that of the "big men" whom he previously despised. Commenting on Museveni's reformation from a Marxist rebel to a self-serving leader, Muhumuza wrote:

> Uganda's president came to power in 1986 as an idealistic former Marxist rebel who denounced power-hungry African leaders. Nearly three decades later, President Yoweri Museveni is now accused by some in the opposition — and others who served prominently under him — of becoming the type of politician he once despised.

> Museveni travels the world in a private jet paid for by taxpayers and recently added two new Mercedes Benz limousines to his convoy. Some say he wants to rule for life, while others worry that Museveni, in the style of some other African strongmen, is trying to groom his son as the country's future leader. That charge was given credence by the defection last month of an army general who urged an investigation into reports of an alleged plot for the first son to succeed his father.[32]

The influence of regressive attitudes toward power remains so strong in contemporary black Africa that even the most well-meaning leaders may eventually be swayed from the progressive course they set for their nations, and revert to the self-serving protectionism that has plagued much of the continent since independence was won from colonial rulers.

The desire to hold onto power as long as possible can be found in every type of organization formed by black Africans—even those who have moved abroad in the diaspora. Since they are socialized under systems that lack accountability, transparency, and fairness, their habits and attitudes reflect this approach to social conduct, and they may still adhere to it when engaging with fellow countrymen abroad. The cultural influence of their host country may have little mitigating effect on this behavior, which is internalized and therefore very difficult to shed.

Anecdote #: 5. A Firm Grip on Power

A group of Nigerian expatriates in the US formed a sociocultural organization to promote members' interests at home and abroad. The founding members were highly educated, some holding doctoral degrees. The group instinctively granted leadership to the most educated members, who assumed the positions of president, vice president, and general secretary.

Over the course of the years, these leaders rotated the positions of power among themselves, and maintained absolute control over every aspect of the organization. Some members expressed discomfort with the arrangement, but the majority acquiesced. On the 10th anniversary of the organization's establishment, the quiet rumblings of discontent erupted into a full-blown crisis that threatened to break up the group. Members openly challenged the officers, calling for a change in leadership and in the direction of the organization.

However, instead of adapting to the change in circumstances and heeding the will of the majority, the leaders fortified their grip on power. It seemed they could not envision a future for the organization without themselves at the helm and never groomed others to succeed them. When opinions strongly diverged about the direction of the organization, the leaders withdrew and the organization collapsed.

The "big man" mentality

In black African political culture, the flawed model of leadership without accountability is rooted in an elitist attitude that is nurtured from the cradle. A "big man," "oga," or "madam" mentality underpins this deeply embedded social dysfunction. African elite families cultivate a psychology of class superiority in their children, surrounding them with servants who attend to all their needs from infancy through secondary school. The children's assumption of privilege is reinforced daily as they witness the debasement of servants and others as social inferiors, and contrasted by the deferential treatment their parents receive in return, even from school teachers and principals. Children of privilege internalize these oppressive values from an early age, and begin to view themselves as miniature executives, or "big men," "big women," and "madams." Their privileged status guarantees them entry into universities, where they will be awarded degrees in prestigious fields such as engineering, medicine, architecture, and law, which will further fortify their superior social standing.

After graduation, these budding elites are immediately offered senior positions in the public or private sectors, and their social conditioning is then complete. Many of these young men and women enter the workforce, not as productive and effective executives, managers, or public officials, but as overpaid and underperforming members of the elite ruling class. Nothing in their privileged upbringing prepares them to apply their knowledge as responsible professionals. Their elevated status easily secured, they push the boundaries of social pretention by appending grand titles to their names, or even creating new titles where none exist. They apply their energy to plotting how they can convert organizational resources to satisfy their own personal needs, and dominate their "social inferiors," who can only nourish a shred of hope that someday it will be their turn to enjoy life as a "big man," "oga," or "madam."

The African "big man" syndrome has not gone unnoticed by the rest of the world. In 2001, *Newsweek* reporter Jeffrey Bartholet described the phenomenon in an article entitled, "A Big Man in Africa," in which he related his experience of interviewing former Liberian leader Charles Taylor.

> Africa is littered with Big Men who fell hard. Some were assassinated, like Laurent Kabila of Congo, who was shot in the head in January by a bodyguard pretending to whisper something in his ear. Others died in mysterious circumstances, like Nigeria's Sani Abacha, who reportedly expired during a Viagra-fueled orgy with prostitutes. Others were chased into ignominious exile, or cling to power against a growing clamor of criticism, like Zimbabwe's Robert Mugabe. But still they come, with their supersize egos, their entourage of sycophants, their penchant for violence. Some have presided over systems so corrupt that they've given rise to

new political terms—like "kleptocracy" and "vampire state."
They plunder the continent's natural resources and leave little in
their wake but ruin. Who are these leaders and what are they
thinking?[33]

The sense of outrage voiced in this description may be felt throughout
the population of nations controlled by such tyrannical figures, but common people who are subject to the whims of autocratic "big man" rulers
generally feel no power to defy their authority. Thus the only opposition
the big men face is from others who wish to claim the same exaggerated
power for themselves.

Leadership and imagined magic – the power of belief

Leadership in black Africa is considered to have a mystical or
magical component, and leaders are widely thought to wield supernatural powers, which add to their aura of invincibility. During the
Nigerian-Biafran civil war, rumors circulated claiming that the
Biafran leader Chukwuemeka Odumegwu Ojukwu, had magically
appeared and disappeared at the battle front. On the federal side of
this brutal civil war, the notoriety of Colonel Adekunle Fajuyi was
likewise attributed in part to his supposed mystical powers. To reinforce the influence of such superstitious beliefs, leaders may engage
in ritual practices that strengthen their magical credentials in the eyes
of their followers.

Professor Florence Bernault from the University of Wisconsin at
Madison, an expert on the history and contemporary politics of Equato-
rial Africa, described this phenomenon in her notes entitled, "Magical
Politics in Equatorial Africa:"

At the twentieth century's end, religion and magic constitute one of the most powerful rhetorics of political
culture in Equatorial Africa. Public rumors depict sor-
cery as the most common way to achieve personal success, wealth, and prestige in times of economic
shortage and declining social opportunities. Political
leaders are widely believed to perform ritual murder to
ensure electoral success and power, and many skillfully

use these perceptions to build visibility and deference.[34]

From the perspective of a modern Western democratic society, this vision of political power and practice seems indescribably remote. This is an indication of how far many black African nations must come before they can hope to enjoy the benefits of functional political systems based on constitutional law and a representative electoral process in which all citizens have a fair and equal voice.

Leadership defined by ethnicity – exploiting the lowest common denominator

It is a widely accepted fact that political power in Sub-Saharan Africa is largely maintained through networks of ethnic allegiance based on tribal membership. Even in urban environments, where little or nothing remains of the original conditions in which tribalism evolved as a social structure, black Africans feel strongly bound to one another through tribal connections. Where members of more than one ethnic group must coexist, leaders are often chosen based on tribal affiliation, and the majority population can wield great power over others in the same region or community.

Both elected and appointed leaders can exploit this deeply engrained tradition of ethnic loyalty and chauvinism, by appealing to the tribal instinct that remains strong in black Africans long after they leave the village behind. This can sharpen existing divisions between rival groups, and cause dangerous rifts that destabilize local populations while concentrating power among the majority ethnic group. It is an effective means of maintaining control, but it reduces any element of the democratic process to a travesty, since tribal affiliation has nothing to do with political opinion or moral principles. The resulting systems of government can never be truly representative, as long as the population governed consists of more than one tribal group.

Since the Sub-Saharan region was divided using borders that cut across tribal boundaries and united inimical groups under the same flags of nationhood, all black Africans must learn to overcome tribal differences if the nations they inhabit are ever to become functioning democratic states. Leaders who exploit tribal divisions are playing to the lowest common denominator in modern African societies, and driving their people backward into a bloody past. Contrast the predominant leadership patterns in black Africa with leadership that can establish effective democratic institutions that allow citizens to shape their societies according to shared principles and common needs, with those who rise above considerations of ethnic origin, and embrace the ideal of ensuring equal rights and opportunities for all citizens as unified nations.

Power and the pursuit of personal wealth

Many Africans in positions of power promote a perverse vision of leadership that equates the attainment of political office with access to a limitless source of personal material wealth. A majority of these leaders pursue power with Machiavellian intent, establishing or maintaining undemocratic systems with the aim of enriching themselves and their cohorts. The unbridled pursuit of power and wealth by black African leaders has deterred investment and economic development, as funds are routinely diverted from the public domain, and the resulting environment of political corruption discourages reputable foreign investors who would practice fair and transparent trade.

As President Emeritus of the World Peace Foundation Robert I. Rotberg wrote in his article, "Good leadership is Africa's missing ingredient," in 2013:

> A majority of the countries of Sub-Saharan Africa are still controlled by men who are motivated not by what they can do for their people but by what their people can do for them. Such leaders exist to prey on their own citizens, to extract from the body politic corrupt rents and other privileges that benefit the ruler and ruling class, their families, and their cliques or lineages. Presidents such as Robert Mugabe in Zimbabwe, Teodoro Obiang Nguema Mbasogo in Equatorial Guinea and Isaias Afewerki in Eritrea are tyrants, but even some of the more moderate of Africa's leaders, like Yoweri Museveni in Uganda, exercise power primarily for themselves and their close ethnic associates, not for the entire nation.[35]

With black African governments corrupted from the top down, greed becomes the operating principle upon which societies are constructed, and dishonesty supplants the rule of law.

Tolerance of corruption at the grassroots

Discussions about corruption in Africa often focus on politicians or political leaders, but corruption is far more embedded in society than acknowledged. It includes teachers, who award passing grades based on sexual favors, beer parlor operators, who rely on looted public funds for their booming businesses; office clerks, who hide files until they receive bribes, officials who inflate or pad invoices to make some money; village chiefs who receive payout for rigging elections; and family members who pressure their sons and daughters to make money while in office and not miss the opportunity of a lifetime. This pervasive corruption is a huge burden that inhibits progress.

Widespread mismanagement – the costs of incompetence and inefficiency

In addition to the drain on resources caused by outright corruption and fraud, many publicly funded programs suffer from inefficient management by those entrusted with these programs. Officials at every level of government and every field of public service often lack the requisite expertise and experience to complete the tasks they are assigned, and nepotism or protectionism may keep inept public servants in office, despite repeated failures. Projects designed to improve the quality of life for rural or urban citizens can falter due to mismanagement and incompetence. Repeatedly, educational initiatives aimed at preventing deadly diseases, providing employment and programs designed to develop and manage local resources, and community efforts of every kind grind to a halt, leaving facilities half built, and debts or salaries unpaid.

CNN Correspondent Robyn Curnow described this phenomenon in reference to a book by South African academic Greg Mills, (*Why Africa is Poor – and What Africans Can Do about It*).

> All of us who live in Africa can name leaders—from presidents to local municipal workers—who have made their communities poorer. It's not just the Mugabes or Mobutus

of this continent who have shattered Africa's promise, it is the often nameless, mid-level workers whose corrupt or incompetent actions result in schoolchildren not getting books, for example.[36]

Since bad management practices are the norm throughout the administrative and social structures of most black African nations, it can be hard for committed local or regional organizers to know where to begin addressing the problems that continually accrue, frustrating all efforts at reform and resolution.

Where public and private interests and enterprise intersect - as in the cultivation or extraction of raw materials - wide-scale mismanagement of funds and resources can destroy a region's best hope for advancement. This is one reason why so many black Africans live in abject poverty, though surrounded by enormous natural wealth that is the envy of even the most highly developed nations. Profitable exploitation of natural resources requires careful planning and execution by skilled and experienced professionals, as well as visionary support by political and financial leaders at the local, state, and national levels.

Failure of leadership among educated black Africans

The African intelligentsia has done little to alter the perilous course of modern African nations. Many university professors not only succumb to the allure of the power and wealth afforded by their elite positions, but implicitly tolerate the moral corruption of those who attain unearned and undeserved leadership roles. Instead of championing equal opportunity in education and professional life, they help to propagate the oppressive models of patriarchy, forced dependency, and pernicious self-interest.

The pervasive lack of leadership in higher education can only deepen the crisis in black African intellectual development—a priceless commodity that represents the only hope for success in modern technology-rich societies. Godwin Murunga, an officer of the African Leadership Center, describes the dismal state of contemporary black African seats of higher learning:

Our intellectual communities are fragmented, dispersed, neglected and ridiculed. The knowledge they produce is often ignored and hardly canonised. It cannot therefore occupy its rightful place in the libraries or in the policy domains where it is urgently and seriously needed.[37]

Without thorough academic preparation at high-quality African colleges, universities, and institutes, the leaders of tomorrow can only repeat the failures of yesterday, instead of preparing the road for urgent progress.

Cold War legacy on African perceptions of leadership

Any analysis of African attitudes toward the roles of leadership and government must weigh the influence of Cold War politics on African development in the post-colonial era. During the second half of the 20th century, newly liberated African nations became the focus of intense competition between capitalist Western nations and the newly formed Union of Soviet Socialist Republics (USSR), with both sides seeking to expand and consolidate their spheres of influence. The socialist ideals promulgated by the U.S.S.R attracted many followers among the first generation of independent African leaders, many of whom equated the colonialist exploitation of their continent with the modern capitalist approach toward development of natural and human resources. Meanwhile, the U.S. and Western European interests supported African leaders who rejected the tenets of the soviet socialist doctrine, which included nationalization of private enterprise. The two opposing sides poured enormous resources into African development, through financial investment, technology transfer, and military support.

Though much of this support never reached the general public in the form of social, economic development or improvements in life quality, the effects of Western and Soviet intervention on the distribution and perception of power in Africa were profound and lasting. Leaders who believed in a socialist approach, or a hybrid of socialism and capitalism (some models distinctly characterized as African), were opposed by those who preferred a capitalist model that allowed for immediate profit from exploitation of natural resources, even if the benefits were not necessarily intended for distribution among the general populace. Since social and political structures were not yet in place to manage the transition to either form of independent government, most leaders failed to achieve their long-term goals, or create stable societies of any kind.

When the Cold War ended, so did the competition it had created for political and economic influence over the new African nations. Many leaders and governments formerly supported by Western and Soviet interests were removed from office, and expectations rose for the establishment of viable indigenous political parties led by strong, committed black Africans. But a half century later, there is little evidence of success in this regard. The public harbors a residual distrust of politicians in general, and a sense of powerlessness to challenge indigenous despots and exploitive foreign players alike.

Blaming outside influence for leadership failures

It is an undisputed fact that black Africa has suffered an immense burden from invasion, colonization, oppression and exploitation by other peoples and nations, not only over the past 500 years, but throughout recorded history. However, since every nation on the continent has now been independent for at least a half century, support is waning for claims by black African leaders that the failures of their regimes and administrations can be ascribed to residual effects of past wrongs committed by foreign powers. Today, increasing numbers of black Africans are calling for accountable and representative leadership from those who hold positions of power in their national and local governments.

The weight of the past is a heavy burden, and one that can never truly be laid down; it must be carried by future generations in the form of wisdom painfully won. But the wrongs of the past can no longer be used as a default excuse for ineffectual or abusive leadership by indigenous Africans, who should be motivated by pride and confidence in the resilience of their people, and inspire them to overcome past failures. Greg Mills wrote the following on why Africa is poor:

> The main reason why Africa's people are poor is because their leaders have made this choice.

> The record shows that countries can grow their economies and develop faster if leaders take sound decisions in the

national interest. Success in the global economy has not required a miracle, an elixir. Good examples to learn from abound, from Vietnam to Costa Rica to Georgia. African leaders face particularly difficult challenges; no one could dispute that. Yet in other parts of the world they are usually regarded as obstacles to be overcome, not as permanent excuses for failure.[38]

Post-colonial black African leadership – a trail of broken promises

Following a massive wave of decolonization during the last half of the 20th century, modern Africa now boasts a total of 54 independent nations.[39] Ghana gained independence in 1957, and its success spurred the rest of black Africa to pursue independence from its European occupiers. From 1957 to 1968, 33 black African countries were decolonized or won their independence. Dr. Nkrumah's victory in Ghana served as an inspiration to all Africans. Other leaders followed - Dr. Nnamdi Azikiwe and Sir Abubakar Tafawa Balewa of Nigeria, Julius Nyerere of Tanzania, Milton Obote of Uganda, Kenneth Kaunda of Zambia; Patrice Lumumba of the Democratic Republic of the Congo, and Robert Mugabe of Zimbabwe. These leaders promised black Africa that the 20th century would be the century of African greatness—an age in which it would achieve untold economic, political, and industrial power—and all this would be accomplished completely free from colonial control, by Africans for Africa.

Since gaining independence, black African countries have experienced multiple crises, including civil wars, political instability, famine, economic stagnation, ethnic conflicts, and regional wars. The impact of the ensuing political instability has lasted for more than 30 years. In addition, the leadership landscape in black Africa has been overshadowed by reports of leaders who chose the path of dictatorship, brute force, human rights abuses, corruption, and mismanagement of their nation's resources.

Leadership experts Jim Kouzes and Barry Posner tell wrote: "Just as architects make drawings and engineers build models, leaders find ways of giving expression to collective hopes for the future."[40] Sadly, this kind of leadership has not been seen in Africa since the likes of Kwame

Nkrumah, Julius Nyerere, Leopold Sedar Senghor, Patrice Lumumba, Jomo Kenyatta, Nnamdi Azikiwe, Obafemi Awolowo, and other seminal post-colonial leaders left the stage.

At the end of World War II, in 1945, nearly every country in Africa (with the exception of Liberia and Ethiopia) was still under colonial rule. Instead of actualizing the vision of these founding fathers, subsequent African leaders—most of whom were thrust into positions of power through coups d'état that subverted the democratic process—have squandered the opportunities they were given for societal transformation, and so betrayed the hopes and aspirations of their people.

As Africa rises from the dark shadows of the past and into the twenty-first century, there are signs of hope. Democracy is once again laying its foundation in black African countries, and authoritarian rule is giving way to democratically elected leaders. A new generation of Africans are demanding accountable leadership, sound economic policies and a break from the proprietary leadership practices of the past. It remains to be seen if this wave of democratically elected leaders will stir their nations and build lasting democratic institutions.

CHAPTER 6

The Socioeconomic Burdens of Black Africa

"People say that if you find water rising up to your ankle, that's the time to do something about it, not when it's around your neck."

Chinua Achebe.

The history of Africa's socioeconomic underdevelopment is fraught with the irony of untold wealth buried deep in the land. Africa is rich in natural and human resources, yet in the eyes of the world, it is always associated with images of extreme poverty, recurring famine, and endless streams of foreign aid that seem to pour into a bottomless pit. It is estimated that African land contains half of the world's gold reserves and a third of the world's diamonds[41] and it is rich in essential minerals and metals such as copper, tin and uranium. The continent also ranks high in oil and gas reserves, as well as timber and agricultural products. Yet the benefits of all this wealth are felt by few of its citizens, due to improper management of resources, production and finance.

For over a century, the cornerstones of African economies have been mineral extraction, trade of other raw materials, and exotic tourism. Unfortunately, after decades of dependence on these natural resources as primary drivers of economic activity, African nations are still clustered near the bottom of the global economic scale. The Gross National Income (GNI) of Sub-Saharan Africans is among the lowest in the world, at less than $765 per person,[42] and most countries in the region also have the lowest ranking in surveys of human development.[43] An estimated 90 percent of Africa's arable land has not been cultivated,[44] which helps explain the continent's marginal contribution to world food production. Variability of climate, antiquated farming methods, lack of access to capital, and poor storage facilities are among the factors that have contributed to the low agricultural output. According to the World Bank, Africa now produces less per person than it did in 1960, though it contains 60 percent of the world's uncultivated arable land.[45] The continent also trails the rest of the world in the manufacture of industrial goods. The stunning irony of black Africa's inability to feed itself is that most of the food consumed in Sub-Saharan Africa is grown locally. So why black Africa continues to look to the west for food is perplexing. The following comments by Nigeria's President, Muhammadu Buhari, highlights how much of Africa's meager foreign reserves are wasted on food importation and the mystery surrounding it:

> I asked, where are the savings? There were none. Where are the railways? The roads? Power? None. I further asked, what did we do with billions of dollars that we made over the years? They said we bought food. Food with billions of dollars? I did not believe, and still do not believe.

> "In most parts of Nigeria, we eat what we grow. People in the South eat tubers, those in the North eat grains, which they plant, and those constitute over 60 percent of what we eat. So, where did the billions of dollars go? We did a lot of damage to ourselves by not developing infrastructure when we had the money.[46]

To address this problem, the Nigerian government, in partnership with private companies, is investing in local production of rice and other staples to steam depletion of its foreign reserves from massive importation of foods that can be produced locally. The way out of Africa's chronic food shortage crisis is local production, by supporting farmers and companies with loans, better-quality seedlings, fertilizer and education on improved farming methods.

Fundamentals for development

A functioning free-market economic system relies not only on balanced forces of supply and demand, but also on a foundation of interpersonal and institutional trust, investor and consumer confidence, and solid legal frameworks that protect individual and property rights and offer a means of seeking redress when these rights are violated. In his remarks at the Reinventing Government Conference in 1999, former World Bank President James D. Wolfensohn, noted that development and reformation efforts can only succeed where four crucial structures coexist—good governance and functioning justice, financial and social systems. He concluded that a country lacking any one of these four elements is "like a rowboat with a big hole in it."[47] Until black Africa undergoes a structural and cultural transformation that will enable its nations to accumulate productive and intangible capital, economic growth cannot be sustained and the current level of continent-wide economic dysfunction will persist. To put it in starker terms, African countries that cannot develop these fundamental support systems are doomed to fail.

Inadequate focus on developing intangible capital

As noted previously in this book, Africa has an abundance of natural resources, but transforming them into material wealth requires diverse skill sets and rigorous mental conditioning that most black Africans do not acquire in their schooling, training, and socialization. In order to provide maximum value, a nation's resources must be managed by efficient public institutions staffed with well-trained personnel who can ensure that production and distribution methods remain efficient—and this presupposes an environment of good governance with sound fiscal policies. More broadly, the effective exploitation of natural resources requires a complex network of, political, economic, and social systems that mutually support each other for the benefit of the nation as a whole.

Underpinning the economic strength of rich nations is the knowledge and skill of their citizens, the quality of their institutions, and the stability and security of their business environment. A 2006 World Bank[48] survey showed that in developed countries, such as the United States of America and Japan, natural resources account for about 3 percent of overall wealth, and productive capital (comprising machinery and infrastructure) is 17 percent. The remaining 80 percent of the overall wealth of rich nations derives from "intangible capital," meaning the knowledge, security, and social stability that allow for productive development. Africa has substantial reserves of natural capital, but it lacks the productive and intangible capital that are crucial for sustainable economic success.

Nigeria is a prime example of a country with large reserves of natural and human capital, but little of the intangible capital described in the World Bank report. The political and economic climate is unsuitable for investment—corruption is pervasive, security is a serious concern, and the cost of doing business is high. Companies that take on the risk of operating in this environment must transfer these costs to local consumers, a majority of whom live on less than $2 a day. Because of the prevalence of bribery and various forms of fraud such as "advance fee fraud," or "419 fraud" as it is known in Nigeria, entrepreneurs must confront an extremely negative stereotype while pitching their business proposals to potential foreign investors. Named after the article of the Nigerian criminal code that applies to fraud, the "419" email-based advanced-fee scam has severely damaged the reputation of the country where it is believed to originate. In a typical internet scam scenario, fraudsters hack into the email account of the potential victim and send an email to everyone listed in the contact folder, soliciting financial assistance under the pretext of a severe health crisis suffered while traveling. The message often claims that the sender is stranded abroad and had lost cash, credit card, or cell phone, and needs an urgent wire transfer of money in order to pay hospital bills before the perpetrator can return home.

This type of email-based fraud has become common. Unfortunately, some are taken in by the scam, and may send large sums of money to the perpetrator, thinking that they are helping someone in need. Though messages of this kind may also be sent from con-artists in other African countries or on other continents, they have become associated with Nigerians.

Since this type of fraud has been widely publicized as a Nigerian phenomenon in the global media, all Nigerians have been tarred with the same brush, and the resulting stigma depletes the nation's intangible capital. Functioning under a cloud of ill repute, Nigerians are challenged to attract the type of investment that will ensure sustained economic growth and improved standard of living for 160 million of its citizens. The negative image resulting from this type of scam underscores the importance of building a strong national reputation as a favorable business environment, which is a fundamental element of a country's overall wealth.

The power of public perception

Negative images perceived and recorded by outsiders is a critical element of black Africa's socioeconomic burden. Reports of corruption, public officials requesting huge kickbacks, lack of infrastructure and social demands on companies make it extremely difficult for entrepreneurs to invest in Africa. Many foreign investors are discouraged from making even an initial visit by the overwhelming flow of media imagery revealing rampant poverty, sickness, and conflict throughout black Africa.

The global NGO Oxfam has attempted to address negative perceptions of black Africa created by media imagery and reporting, and by the portrayals of poverty, famine, and conflict that are used to generate donations from abroad. An article from the British news outlet, *The Guardian*, describes the effects of the constant stream of imagery that almost exclusively depicts adverse conditions:

> When we asked a random selection of 2,000 people across the UK what they think of when they think of Africa, more than half said "poverty", "famine" and "hunger". Only a small percentage said growth, business, education, or landscapes.
>
> Respondents described the stereotypical portrayal of Africa as "depressing, manipulative and hopeless", with 43% of people asked saying it made them feel that conditions in the developing world would never improve. Three out of five of those polled said they were or had become desensitised to images depicting issues such as hunger, drought and disease and almost one in four (23%) admitted they turned away when confronted by such images.[49]

Oxfam's revised approach is to feature images of Africa's natural beauty in their reports on regions that remain in need of support, while also describing progress that has been achieved in recent years. The goal is to change foreigners' perspective toward a continent they may know only through the negative images to which they have been exposed through news reports and charity campaigns.

While some may not agree with this approach, which can be seen as minimizing the full impact of Africa's socioeconomic difficulties, it does address an important question about the power of media imagery to influence public attitudes. In the current globalized environment of diversified media access, people around the world are constantly invited to form opinions based on little more than a retouched photograph and a sound bite from a popular celebrity. Well-balanced and unbiased news reports are often available for those who take the time to review the issues in depth, but the vast majority of media consumers accept the images presented to them at face value, and look no further.

As black Africans join forces to alter their collective destiny for the better, taking control of their own image can help them to claim their pride of place in the global collage. When media consumers from abroad see frequent reports on infrastructural development efforts, urban renewal projects, improvements in health and education services, and successful entrepreneurial ventures, they will begin to perceive Sub-Saharan Africa as an attractive destination for travel and a worthy venue for collaborative investment. Since positive developments of this kind may not be considered newsworthy to foreign media outlets, the responsibility for representing these aspects of African life to the world will rest with Africans themselves.

Building castles on sand – growth spurts unsupported by fundamentals

Until the great recession of 2008, economic forecasts offered an optimistic outlook for some black African economies. They were reported to be growing at higher rates than those of Europe and America, and were reportedly expanding faster than almost any other region of the world. But Africa has witnessed false dawns, cycles of economic boom, and devastating busts before, and the growth spurt was based on the same weak structural foundation that failed to support so many past dreams and plans. Due to the shaky foundation on which those economies were based, they could not withstand the shock of the great recession. In addition, the expansion in production and trade was driven primarily by external forces, while Africans played at the margins, and few benefits trickle down to the vast majority of the population.

Modern Africa has long basked in the glow of its potential greatness and the promise of a better future, but the bright portrait painted by some analysts does not include the backdrop of poverty, malnutrition, national debt, dependence on foreign aid, epidemic disease, dilapidated infrastructure, lack of skilled labor, political instability, and socially embedded corruption that still characterize the nations whose economies were said to be booming. Past cycles of economic growth have never translated into improved standards of living for the majority of African citizens, and so far, the boom in the opening decades of the twenty-first century was not different. Though many African nations now boast a budding middle class, these eager new consumers can easily be thrown back into penury by the wild swings that often characterize developing economies. The new African middle class is built on a shaky foundation, and its buying power alone cannot be relied upon as the engine to drive future economic development. Nigerians often gloat about their individual achievements at home and abroad. Commenting on the need to reverse the high number of Nigerian professionals abroad, Michel Arrion, the EU Ambassador to Nigeria and the Economic Community of West African States (ECOWAS) noted that there are more Ph.D. holders, medical doctors and nurses of Nigerian origin in Europe and the U.S. than in Nigeria.[50] It is estimated that more than 21,000 Nigerian doctors were practicing in the U.S.; the numbers are staggering if those in Europe, Australia, the Middle East, and other countries are included. The statistics are impressive and indeed something that arouses a sense of pride. But these achievements have not been channeled as resources for development. Nigeria, with the largest concentration of black people in the world, implicitly bears a responsibility to demonstrate that black Africans can build a thriving modern developed nation. Princeton N. Lyman, the former U.S. Ambassador to Nigeria and South Africa, said the following about Nigerian's focus on its strategic importance:

> Let me sort of deconstruct those elements of Nigeria's importance, and ask whether they are as relevant as they have been. We

often hear that one in five Africans is a Nigerian. What does it mean? Do we ever say one in five Asians is a Chinese? Chinese power comes not just for the fact that it has a lot of people but it has harnessed the entrepreneurial talent and economic capacity and all the other talents of China to make her a major economic force and political force.

What does it mean that one in five Africans is Nigerian? It does not mean anything to a Namibian or a South African. It is a kind of conceit. What makes it important is what is happening to the people of Nigerian. Are their talents being tapped? Are they becoming an economic force? Is all that potential being used?[51]

Putting Nigeria's size and economic crisis in context, Aubrey Hruby wrote in *Newsweek* that,

Instead of debating relative size, Nigerian officials and those with business interests in the country need to focus on working through the short-term economic pain of much-needed reforms. Now is the time to lay the foundation for a more sustainable, diversified long-term period of growth.[52]

Nigeria's development and progress could serve as bacon for black pride and fulfillment. Only if individual achievements of black people can be challenged to lift Africa's burden, can Africans proclaim they have come of age.

Strong economies are sustained by a constant drive to innovate, engineer solutions and produce quality goods and services efficiently, with sound distribution and supply chain management systems that distribute goods widely to a solid consumer base. Industrialization has enabled the development of mass production, and manufacturing has been the primary source of rapid and continuing economic growth in the world's emerging economies. But Africa has yet to make the transition from low to high productivity; instead, there has been a substantial regression from the initial post-independence push for industrialization.

The United Nations Conference on Trade and Development (UNC-TAD), African Development Report for 2012 indicated that manufacturing output fell by 2 percent in North Africa between 1990 and 2008, East Africa witnessed a decline of 3 percent; Central and South Africa saw manufacturing output drop by 5 percent, while West Africa saw the steepest fall of 8 percent.[53] The reason for this near-universal decline in manufacturing is that African governments have not established productivity-enhancing economic and social constructs to drive steady growth. As the UNCTAD report suggests, "If African countries want to achieve high and sustained economic growth, they have to go through the process of structural transformation involving an increase in the share of high productivity manufacturing and modern services in output, accompanied by an increase in agricultural productivity and output."[54]

Fixed social attitudes – a drag on growth and productivity

At the heart of Africa's socioeconomic burden is a cultural orientation that has been difficult to transform—a pervasive system of beliefs, customs, and attitudes that prevent countries from enhancing their economic prowess. In essence, black Africa has nurtured a culture that subverts its own advancement. Existing value systems do not support modern high-volume productivity, and black African nations have not been able to build financial and civic structures that will encourage the required change in focus. The prevailing socioeconomic attitudes and behaviors seem to be locked in a self-destructive dance of mutual inhibition.

As an example, let us consider the economic implications of African social attitudes toward time. Africans are generally known to have a fluid conception of time, untrammeled by any emphasis on punctuality or efficiency of effort. This culturally-based tendency has serious implications for productivity in the highly competitive and rapidly changing global economy. In today's integrated worldwide market, time is of the essence, as production and delivery of goods depend on precisely choreographed schedules. A system of production based on the subjective African attitude toward time is likely to produce disastrous results for the business interests involved.

Furthermore, many Africans still view modernization as alien, and they mistrust and disapprove of the processes involved in the transformation of natural resources such as oil, iron ore, gold, and other precious minerals into material wealth. A story widely narrated, among friends in the Midwest and Eastern regions of Nigeria, on social occasions, illustrates how certain customs impede development and how deadly the consequences of ignorance can be. Mr. Nwapuda, an indigene of Umuahia, opposed the construction of a rail line through his inherited land. He swore trains will only pass through his land over his dead body. Government authority prevailed and the rail track was constructed across a portion of Mr. Nwapuda's land, but he continued to insist that no train would pass his land. His opposition to the rail line was so strong that when Mr Nwapuda, heard a train approaching, he stretched himself across the rail racks and was tragically crushed when the train rolled over him. Fact or fiction, Mr. Nwapuda's story illustrates how customs and ignorance impose challenges for development projects.

Certain perceptions also manifest as dysfunctional attitudes toward work in the modern sense, and the result has been a stereotyped view of African workers as prone to laziness, recklessness, waste, and fraud. This perceived bad attitude toward modern work has posed an enduring dilemma for African entrepreneurs, and it can have devastating consequences for individuals who try to make the leap from paid employment to small business ownership.

Anecdote # : 6. An African Entrepreneur

Mr. Amari lived in the United States and supported his extended family in West Africa with regular financial remittances. As the number of his dependents and their demands increased, Amari's income was stretched to the limit. With the pressure on his resources continually mounting, he realized that sending money home only reinforced his relatives' sense of dependency, and encouraged them to ask for more instead of developing their own potential.

In order to remedy the situation, Amari decided to purchase a van for one of his unemployed male cousins to operate as a transport vehicle, so he could earn his own living. A preliminary survey confirmed that the business would generate enough income to cover running costs, support his cousin, and allow him to undertake other ventures, so Mr. Amari purchased and shipped a suitable van back home.

Before shipping the van, Amari had several discussions with his cousin about the operation of the new business, and the potential benefits that would accrue to the whole family. To ensure that the business would run smoothly, Mr. Amari even traveled back to Africa to help get it started. He saw to it that the vehicle cleared customs, and proudly presented the keys to his cousin. The event was celebrated with a small ceremony, in which Amari's father and the village elders offered traditional prayers for the success of the business.

However, as many who have ventured to start a new business in Africa have experienced, Mr. Amari soon ran into multiple difficulties. Barely a month after his return to the US he received a call from his cousin, and the news was grim— apparently, the vehicle had developed engine trouble. The nature of the problem was described in mysterious terms, capped with "we are putting everything in God's hands"—a statement that signals resignation and failure to anyone who has regular dealings with African entrepreneurs. After several follow-up calls, Amari was informed that the engine needed to be completely overhauled, although a mechanic had checked and certified the vehicle before it was purchased. Amari was told that the cost of the repairs would equal the original costs of acquiring and shipping the van.

Amari was devastated; he had spent all his savings and had taken a cash advance from his credit card to fund the venture, and now he was left to pay the debt without any proceeds from the business. To add insult to injury, he subsequently learned that the story about the vehicle's engine trouble had been concocted by his cousin to make him abandon the project, so that his cousin could sell the van and keep the proceeds. Reeling from the loss and from his sense of personal betrayal, Mr. Amari vowed never to do business again with anyone at home and from then on, he restricted his cash remittances only to his parents.

The scenario described in this anecdote is quite typical of family business ventures in black Africa—a perfect example of best intentions colliding with ignorance about the basic principles of business, trade, or commerce. It also illustrates the dysfunctional attitude of many Africans toward work-unaccustomed to the standards of behavior required for a modern business to succeed, they may seek to maximize their immediate returns and run their business aground. Workers fail to see the connection between the work they are required to do and the potential long-term benefit to their own economic wellbeing. Many black Africans still view employment, in the modern sense, as something foreign and unconnected with their experience; therefore they develop no sense of ownership for their work or the means by which they earn their living. Instead, they may perpetuate systems of dependency that place unsustainable financial burdens on a few breadwinners, who thereby become trapped in financial sinkholes from which there is no escape. Martin Meredith noted in *The Fate of Africa: A History of Fifty Years of Independence,* that: "During the colonial era, many Nigerians regarded government institutions as 'olu oyibo' – Whiteman's business, an alien system that could be plundered when necessary. 'Government business is no man's business,' ran a popular Nigerian saying."[55]

Social conditions that discourage individual initiative

Unfortunately, many talented black Africans are hampered by multiple negative influences: social conditions that discourage individual initiative, a crushing sense of the technological superiority of developed countries, and a paralyzing fear of failure in the challenging modern environment. Encumbered from the start by so many disincentives to act in their own best interests, they fail to see opportunities for advancement. Only the nimblest in adapting to change will manage to meet the new challenges that rush toward them at breakneck speed.

Resistance to developing and sharing of new ideas

The blessing of abundant natural sources of food for self-sustenance has become a curse due to the inability or failure to find creative solutions to maintain availability from generation to generation. Modernity and population growth have altered human lives in a way subsistent living cannot. A majority of black Africans still live in poor, rural communities that rely on subsistence farming. Due to poverty, lack of education, and access to financial resources, people in much of black Africa are unable to devote their time, energy, and other resources to creative experimentation or any endeavor that may involve financial undertaking. Those who are employed, even at subsistence levels, may fear striking out on their own to begin small businesses, or develop original new products or services.

Limited resources and inadequate infrastructure and institutional support inhibit the capacity of most black Africans to package and market innovative ideas, not only for mass consumption but even for the benefit of their local communities. Furthermore, many are hesitant to share or reveal their ideas, for fear of being cheated or losing any advantage they may gain through their creative inspiration. The lack of trust between individuals and within organizations, and the absence of legal mechanisms to protect intellectual property, continue to stifle cooperative development and discourage the profitable dissemination of new products and techniques.

Mistaken priorities – self-gratification trumping development

Another element affecting black African socioeconomic development is the tendency of African businessmen and members of the wealthy elite to gravitate toward personal consumption, with less emphasis on increasing productivity. Many spend a high percentage of their income and business profits on luxury goods, such as high-end automobiles, designer clothing, grand mansions, and expensive trips abroad. Politicians and officials may also loot public funds that could have been invested in business and infrastructure development or other public projects.

Those who achieve power of any kind feel compelled to compete with each other in demonstrating their wealth through conspicuous consumption and maintaining all the trappings of a luxurious lifestyle. For example, men may spend large sums on multiple mistresses, whose demands increase to match the bank accounts of their wealthy lovers.

History shows that nations thrive when governments invest in their people and infrastructure; when they promote multiple export industries, develop a skilled workforce, and offer incentives to small and medium-sized businesses that in turn create jobs. But far too often, corruption and greed have driven developing economies off the rails, as leaders neglect the public good in favor of their own pleasures and personal gain. The result is a generalized failure to thrive that infects every level of society. This creates a sense of powerlessness and insecurity; even those few who manage to achieve success must always live in fear that their wealth will be snatched.

Weak frameworks for cooperation and connection

The socioeconomic dysfunction of black African nations is exacerbated by the insular structures and fortifications of their communities; countries landlocked or demarcated by artificial boundaries, and populations separated by cultural differences or tribal disputes can seem as remote from one another as if they were on different continents. Many black Africans know only those who dwell in their own small enclave or within easy traveling distance and may be barely aware of the countries that border their own, or the people who inhabit those foreign lands. Of course, this lack of awareness or intolerance is reinforced when conflicts break out between neighbors who may be competing for resources or replaying ancient disputes that may no longer have relevance in the modern world.

Naturally, economic development requires functioning basic infrastructure that will allow for reliable communication, transportation of goods and raw materials, and adequate sources of power and water that can be distributed efficiently throughout inhabited areas. Sub-Saharan Africa faces enormous challenges in all of these respects, with substantial deficits in every country in the region. Since infrastructural networks must cross national boundaries, development also requires cooperation between neighboring countries, and peaceful conditions in which to consummate contractual agreements and complete necessary construction projects. Sadly, black Africa is still riven by cross-border and internal conflicts that disrupt attempts to establish reliable networks of transportation, communication, and supplies.

Language barriers can prove just as difficult to breach, and with more than 1,000 different tongues spoken throughout Africa, this can be a daunting obstacle. Communication is essential for economic development, since shared language is the primary foundation of human commerce. Without this basic connection, even at the local level, it is hard to imagine building expandable networks that support national, regional, and international commerce.

Finally, a general lack of infrastructure impedes personal communication and commercial transportation. Limited telephone service, basic utilities, and reliable roads and railways leave vast tracts of Africa unconnected, not only to the outside world, but also to the nearest sources of information, trade, and commerce. Even where these services are available, the cost of access may render them prohibitive to much of the population. However, due to the growing penetration of wireless phone technology, the situation is changing.

Foreign imports – a double-edged sword

Importation of foreign goods and produce appears to offer the easiest solution to the difficulty of providing many basic necessities to African citizens when famine, disease, conflict, and lack of infrastructure hinder the development of local production and innovation. However, this can also feed a vicious cycle of chronic dependence on imports, and failure of indigenous enterprises to thrive. The availability of cheaply manufactured clothing and highly subsidized farm products from around the globe discourages investment in local ventures, which are prone to the risks inherent to any developing economy.

Industrial infrastructure in most black African nations is still stuck at the level of processing and exporting raw materials. The value of raw materials increases as they move up the chain of manufacturing into increasingly refined and sophisticated products. So there is real incentive for establishing African industries to transform local resources before they are exported. For example, raw coffee beans increase in value as they are roasted, packaged, branded, and eventually consumed as brewed beverage in service establishments such as restaurants, cafes, and hotels. With limited local markets for both raw and refined products, Africa loses the lion's share of profit from its own resources. Exporting raw materials, while importing finished goods, can drain national economies, instead of stimulating development. It is the opposite of the process required for economic growth.

Capital flight and illegal transfers

A 2013 report prepared jointly by the African Development Bank (ADB) and Global Financial Integrity (GFI), a research organization dedicated to reducing international traffic of illicit funds, found that, "between 1980 and 2009, the economies of Africa lost between US$597 billion and US$1.4 trillion in net resource transfers away from the continent."[56] While some of these transfers were related to legitimate transactions, the report states that "Illicit financial flows (IFFs) were the main driving force behind the net drain of resources from Africa of US$1.2 - 1.3 trillion on an inflation-adjusted basis."[57] This represents an astounding loss for a region that is already profoundly underdeveloped, and it helps explain the lack of progress in expanding the economic base of black African nations. As the report concludes, "The resource drain on Africa over the past thirty years is almost equivalent to Africa's current GDP. This represents a major drag on African development, and dwarfs much of the effort that donor countries undertake to boost the continent's struggling economies."[58]

Along with criminal trafficking and smuggling of contraband, tax evasion and corruption account for much of capital loss from Africa. Profits from exploitation of natural resources or deliberate mispricing of goods and services are secretly expropriated abroad, for the benefit of a few highly placed and powerful individuals or groups. With few controls on trade and little transparency in business and public spending, it is impossible for citizens and organizations to track this outflow or report on capital losses to the general population.

Without a more rigorous system of management for public finances and commercial enterprise, national wealth will continue to drain from black African nations like water from a leaky tub. It is not just a question of blocking avenues of tax evasion and money laundering, the illicit capital outflow must be stopped at the source, by increasing transparency and oversight of financial transactions, and ensuring that accountability is maintained through accurate and thorough record keeping. These systems are prerequisites for economic development at every level, from local governments to national taxation and allocation of public funds.

Economic migrants – Brain drain

The growing phenomenon of economic migrants has left capacity gaps in many black African countries where their skills and services are needed. Africans who studied abroad before, and immediately following, independence, returned home to spearhead and manage development in their countries. The tide turned dramatically during the dying decades of the 20th century. Much of Africa's intellectual capital fled abroad for better opportunity. Though the drain is compensated, to a degree, by the gain provided through their repatriated earnings, it is not clear that the overall impact on development is positive, and many believe it is actually detrimental. In a paper written for the Southern Africa Migration Project entitled, "Migration, Remittances and Development in Southern Africa," the authors list potential drawbacks:

First, there is the difficulty of converting remittances into sustainable productive capacity. Second, remittance income is rarely used for productive purposes but for direct consumption. Very little is directed to income-earning, job-creating investment. Finally, remittances increase inequality, encourage import consumption and create dependency.[59]

Inadequate functional financial systems

Of course, no nation's economy can show sustainable growth without the support of a solid financial infrastructure, in which investment, lending, and trading can transpire under the protection of sound governmental regulation and oversight. In most black African countries, the necessary systems are extremely underdeveloped, and though recent reforms have offered hope for gradual improvement, the region trails other parts of the world in terms of availability of sophisticated financial systems. The banking and insurance industries are still in their infancy, and newly established stock exchanges have the lowest value of any in the world.

Since maintaining transparency and responsible regulation will be crucial to the efficacy of these financial structures, the challenge will be to avoid compromise or capitulation forced by government agencies that are riddled with corruption. If undemocratic or dishonest administrations manage to rig financial systems for their own interests while neglecting the needs of the general public, the result will be decades of continued economic dysfunction, with all the social ills it can engender.

Shedding dependence and establishing internal drivers for socioeconomic development

The economic growth of any nation must be driven from within, and while foreign donations or investments can help kick-start regional development, they can never sustain the wealth production of an independent nation over the long term. Dependence on external support can actually defer the establishment of indigenous industry, while the lack of public control over resource management and distribution of benefits can divert national wealth for the private gain of unscrupulous profiteers and foreign concerns.

The social and economic aspects of development must proceed hand in hand, as all human commerce depends on networks of communication, collaboration and exchange. Establishing these complex interconnections takes time and effort, and more importantly, a sense of commitment to the process of nation-building, and a positive attitude toward the future. These will be the keys to success for the African nations that can accept the challenges that confront them, and convert their abundant resources for the good of all through productive, creative and collaborative actions.

CHAPTER 7

Political, Social, and Cultural Schisms at Home and Abroad

Unity is more of an understanding, than a construct.

Social fragmentation is one of the heaviest burdens born by black Africans, both at home and abroad. From Praia, Cape Verde, to Mogadishu, Somalia, and Pretoria, South Africa, to Mekele, Ethiopia, there is little or no collaboration in the areas of research, education, health care, commerce, and information exchange. Black Africans in the diaspora have yet to develop and maintain platforms for cooperation among them on a sustained level. The African Union and other regional bodies are more or less symbols rather, than real instruments for cooperation in the advancement of Africa. These organizations have done little beyond the lofty pronouncements in their charters to promote collaboration in education, science, research, commerce, and communication. Similar divisive forces have prevented people in the African diaspora from forging a unified front to tackle Africa's burdens.

The divisive insularity is just as deep-rooted, and this has indirectly stifled development on the continent. Diaspora Africans have amassed enormous human and financial capital that can be channeled to address some of the challenges facing African nations, yet national or tribal loyalty inhibits collaboration and the development of common goals. Tribal identity that has defined black African politics within nations is a force that still drives the behavior of educated Africans living abroad, who otherwise could serve as crucial sources of organizational and financial support for development efforts in their home countries.

Social fragmentation increases vulnerability

When social creatures of any kind are challenged by dangerous conditions, they typically join forces to protect themselves against the common threat. When their very survival is at stake, the need to present a united front becomes a matter of extreme urgency. Unfortunately, this kind of unity has rarely been achieved in black Africa, though the need has long been undeniable. Throughout the 20th century and into the new millennium, a relentless onslaught of natural disasters, famines, pandemics, regional conflicts, and despotic regimes has displaced or killed millions of people, and wreaked havoc on their nations—yet black Africans have failed to close ranks and combat these grave threats as they arise.

The inability to identify and strengthen the ties that unite them has left black African societies at the mercy of circumstance, with no sense of direction or productive union. Cooperation among African nations proceeds by feeble fits and starts, and is often driven by counterproductive motives; instead of joining forces against threats of political or economic repression, African leaders may tacitly collaborate to protect corrupt and oppressive regimes. In one example Muammar Gadhafi of Libya sent 3,000 troops to aid the brutal regime of Ugandan President Idi Amin in 1978.[60] The result this and similar alliances is always an increase in social dysfunction, reduction of freedom and civil rights, and disruption of the lines of communication and commerce without which progress toward economic development in black Africa will remain an impossible dream. By contrast, the decision by the Economic Commission of West African States (ECOWAS) to use military force to oust President Yahya Jammeh of Gambia,[61] in January 2017 and enforce the will of the Gambian people is a testament to the benefits of positive collaboration.

Evolution of black African fragmentation

The complex ethnic and cultural diversity of black African societies have caused deep divisions and intractable conflicts that have lasted for decades, fueled by historical animosity, competition for resources, territorial disputes, and an anachronistic desire to reinforce tribal identity or superiority. Attempts by rebel factions to separate from states to which they feel no allegiance, or to replace dictatorial regimes with democracy and the rule of law, have also resulted in prolonged and bitter fighting. Persistent conflict among black Africans at every social level has had a destabilizing and destructive influence on African societies.

As described in the section on tribalism and superstition, a majority of black Africans still view ethnic affiliation in existential terms, and the tribe as the central unit of social function. They may feel conflicting inclinations, to individuate and compete like modern global citizens, or maintain their privileged traditional social status. However, it is becoming increasingly evident that as black Africans continue the difficult transition toward modernity, the influence of traditional values is beginning to wane, and many who have been socialized with an emphasis on cooperative coexistence have opted for a more individualistic and competitive lifestyle.

In many cases, the pendulum swings too far in the direction of self-interest, and "modernized" black Africans lose all sense of personal responsibility for maintaining the continuity of traditional social structures. Lacking the commitment of individuals to the causes of the community, group communication and cooperation break down at every level. Since healthy, functional and supportive societies cannot be built on fragmented foundations, the resulting lack of social cohesion diminishes the capacity of all black Africans to tackle the myriad problems that confront them as they struggle to adapt to a more modern way of life.

Tribal divisions – a source of modern disunity

Viewed from the outside, black Africa seems to be a region unified by shared disadvantages, and most have little knowledge of the differences among African nations and their distinct ethnic peoples. In contrast, most Africans living on the continent see the world through the eyes of their own local ethnic group, which influences or determines all social, economic, and political alliances. Human and financial resources are rarely pooled to promote successful development projects, as organizations are quickly split by prejudice and self-interest. They are torn apart by their differences, rather than unified by common goals. The resulting cultural insularity stifles the growth of social and economic synergies across ethnic lines.

Ethnic identity is a central issue inhibiting cooperation among black Africans in the diaspora. Though host country citizens could hardly differentiate a Kenyan from a Cameroonian, or Nigerian from a Ghanaian, and few have any knowledge of the different ethnic groups that inhabit these nations, Africans still fail to see their common interests. Most foreigners only become aware of the divisions that separate black Africans along ethnic lines when conflict erupts between factions, and civil or international war occurs. The gruesome news reports that follow damage the image of black Africa in the eyes of the world, and reinforce the image of Africa as a place of brutal, genocidal, primitive warring tribes with barbaric, despotic leaders.

Lack of cooperation among diaspora Africans

A less outwardly visible, but no less destructive, manifestation of African social fragmentation is the ethnic self-segregation of black Africans living abroad. Naturally, people gravitate toward others with whom they feel a sense of shared experience and common cause. But, the groups and organizations formed by black Africans who live and work abroad often reflect the emphasis on tribal affiliation that they have internalized, with all the conflict it engenders. Even if their tribal identity did not serve a central social function for them at home, Africans in diaspora tend to coalesce in groups along ethnic lines, and thus maintain the divisions that have always separated them from most of their fellow countrymen on the continent.

Unfortunately, this tendency toward social fragmentation impedes the efforts of Africans living abroad to improve the lot of those who remain at home. There are various organizations in the diaspora that champion important causes to develop Africa, but there have been few concerted efforts to pull these groups together and pool their resources to maximize their efficiency and positive impact.

Even among their own members, African organizations are often plagued by intense infighting over issues related to fraud, mismanagement, abuse of office, lack of transparency, and other threats to stability and progress. Group efforts may be initiated with the best intentions, but soon after organizations are officially launched, egotistical behaviors rise to the surface, and unity of purpose breaks down under the pressure of competing interests. Officials may channel organizational resources to further their own agendas, which may be hidden or misrepresented. For example, in one organization operating in the U.S., some of the executive officers joined forces to purchase a meeting hall for group events, and one of them offered to lend the organization money to renovate the premises. Though this was represented as an altruistic gesture, the officer secretly tied the loan to his interests such that a portion of the interest paid on the loan allegedly went to him, though he continued to vaunt himself as a grand patron of the organization.

Instead of serving as responsible leaders, officials in African organizations often ignore the bylaws governing their conduct, and proceed according to their own interests and inclinations. If and when their abuses are exposed, the members become embroiled in discord and the organization ceases to function. This pattern exactly reflects the cycle of deception and disillusionment that has stalled most efforts to improve the deplorable conditions under which so many black Africans on the continent struggle to survive.

The roots of self-defeating behavior

The continuing discord among black Africans at home and abroad has mired them in a vicious cycle of mutual animosity and self-destructive behavior. At one extreme are the authoritarian and corrupt leaders, and at the other are followers who overtly (or covertly) resist their authority. This dynamic can be peculiarly destructive when it operates among black Africans living abroad who have reestablished dysfunctional social patterns in their new host countries.

For black Africans who have been socialized in colonial or post-colonial societies, the dynamic can be even more complex, as some may never have accepted their own national identity. Others who differentiate themselves as members of a minority group, tend to revert to the default identity for black Africans, which is their tribal heritage.

When diaspora Africans attempt to organize in any kind of hierarchical social structure, they quickly find themselves hamstrung by reflexive prejudice, and the mistrust and animosity it breeds. Scarred by previous negative experiences, Africans in positions of authority may launch a preemptive strike by dealing with fellow Africans heavy-handedly. Similarly, their subordinates may transfer residual feelings from bad experiences with African authoritarian figures, and react negatively to any African in a superior position. The result can be a toxic environment of reciprocal belligerence and distrust, in which it is impossible to achieve positive progress toward any goal, even if it would benefit all parties involved. In her book, *Rock My Soul: Black People and Self-Esteem*, Bell Hooks explains her view of how black people living as minority members of a white society may reflexively perpetuate the twisted logic of self-hate. She writes:

> The harshness with which they judge black peers is often contrasted with keen willingness to extend to white folks a more generous and compassionate critical evaluation. This harshness is itself a reflection of a racist climate wherein it is deemed acceptable by society to be more judgmental of the actions of black folks, who are often held in higher standards and who are then found wanting... Embracing this ethos, black people are [*perpetually*] placed in adversarial relations to [*themselves*].[62]

Traits that define successful cultures

The perception in the developed world seems to hold that people of African heritage remain poor because they only care about the present day, while Europeans and Asians are able to achieve wealth and success because they invest in the future. The relatively few Africans who possess the initiative and means required to travel abroad for educational and professional experience are certainly investing in their own personal success, but most do not return to the African continent to redeploy the knowledge they have gained for commercial or social development. Of course, many never leave home because they have no resources to devote to their own advancement, and must struggle to survive day-to-day. Likewise, many economic migrants seek subsistence-level jobs in developed countries, where their lack of education, language skills, and racial prejudice may prevent them from achieving a higher socioeconomic status. In any case, rich and poor alike carry the same inherited burden of social fragmentation that limits their ability to connect and cooperate with others in similar circumstances.

Instead of uniting to forge a positive global image, and thus helping to promote important causes that affect millions of black people around the world, black Africans in the diaspora congregate socially in parochial organizations or communities, in which they typically argue amongst themselves and blunder in circles without any sense of commitment or direction.

The failure of black Africans in the diaspora to address urgent issues affecting their people and their homeland can be partially attributed to a realistic fear of investing time, effort and money in risk-laden projects or ventures, and a lack of supporting organizational infrastructure to facilitate development efforts. Many would rather cooperate with partners from Europe or Asia than reach out to fellow Africans. In their eagerness to embrace the middle-class, Western lifestyle, many diaspora Africans gladly imbibe the social values of their adopted countries, swearing never to return home. They have no desire to advance development causes, which they may consider a waste of their personal resources.

Black Africa's best and brightest – falling short as leaders of development

More than a half century after the colonial nations of Africa achieved independence, it remains a deeply fractured continent whose people are filled with fear, envy, and distrust of one another. Many of those who should be leading the way toward a brighter future, including political leaders, teachers, pastors, business people, respected professionals, and students still live as if they were under the control of colonial powers, afraid to take a stand for social change or challenge the status quo.

Most Africans on the continent, and even many in the diaspora, have failed to understand that the globalized nature of the 21st century necessitates cooperation among individuals, communities, and nations. The irony is that black Africans used to be proud of their culture and heritage, grounded in cooperation and collective effort, are unwilling to employ those values to advance African causes. Too many stubbornly adhere to habitual norms of tribalism and ethnic prejudice, which are counter-productive attitudes that impede progress. All black Africans should be driven by the magnitude of the challenges they face to accept the responsibility that history has placed on the present generation of Africans. The challenge black Africans must tackle is to raise the profile and advance the cause of Africa and its people in an increasingly complex global environment, and manage the natural resources of the continent for the benefit of all Africans.

Black Africans who have achieved advanced education and positions of respect and influence in society have the power to promote development and shine the light on the important issues affecting the lives of Africans at home and abroad. Through collaborative partnerships with others who feel a sense of social responsibility and an appreciation for the benefits of community activism, Africans can lead the effort to improve the quality of life for those less fortunate. But how will black Africans use the advantages they have gained to provide help and encouragement to those who have not been blessed with the same opportunities?

Decades after scholar activist W.E.B Dubois[63] placed responsibility for the development of black Africa on the best brains Africa can produce, many seem content with change that happens upon them. If those who have the power and knowledge to lead do not accept the challenge of responsible leadership, there will be little hope of a bright future for the world's black people.

Part

II

CHAPTER 8

Lifting the Burden: The Way Forward

"We owe it to all the peoples of the sub-continent to ensure that
they see in us, not merely good leaders waxing lyrical about development,
but as the front commanders in the blast furnaces of labor,
productive investments and visible change."

Nelson Mandela.

Charting a new path for Africa that will facilitate a transition from the pre-industrial to the information age is a daunting task. The first part of this book has been devoted to describing Africa's burdens candidly, without the defensive shield that often blinds us to reflective insights. It holds up a mirror before the eyes every black African, and the image reflected represents neither who we thought we were, nor who we would like to be. However, defining Africa's problems is only the first (and easiest) part of this journey; devising and implementing enduring solutions that can lighten and eventually lift black Africa's many burdens is a much more challenging prospect.

The chapters that follow offer practical solutions and approaches to address the enormous deficits in development that persist throughout the Sub-Saharan region. It must be acknowledged that the continuing accumulation of Africa's burdens is not for lack of well-crafted blueprints for positive change. Over the years, a cornucopia of development models have been prescribed, attempted, and failed. Programs have been designed to address problems in every sphere of human life and social endeavor, including healthcare, education, nutrition, poverty and debt reduction, gender equality, environmental management, and urban planning. The United Nations, European Union, and governments of many developed countries have provided assistance in every sector where progress lags. Nevertheless, the report card still shows an unflattering portrait of the lives of a majority of black Africans. The United Nations Millennium Development Goals report for 2015 shows that in 1990, 2011, and 2015, Sub-Saharan Africa had the highest proportion of people living on less than $1.25 a day. Sub-Saharan Africa also had the highest proportion of undernourished people in 1990 to 1992 and 2014 to 2016.[64]

This chapter will describe a wide range of micro- and macro-level measures that can help to put Sub-Saharan Africa solidly on the road to sustainable development. This journey will be fraught with dangers, and those who dare to undertake it will encounter unpredictable obstacles and inevitable setbacks along the way. Yet serious effort has been made to offer fresh insights and new approaches to old problems, as well as revisit previous interventions with an open mind and a renewed sense of optimism and common purpose.

CHAPTER 9

Educating Minds, Transforming Attitudes

"A dream doesn't become reality through magic; it takes sweat, determination and hard work."

Colin Powel.

The world of magical reality

In worlds driven by innovation and creativity, people dream and make their dreams a reality – they advance our world through concrete reality. But there is an alternate reality lived in the mind, a world of *magical reality* where people dream of things that never manifest in concrete reality. It is a virtual world of beliefs, unfulfilled dreams and fantasies only those who believe sense.

In the world of concrete reality, humans dreamt of free nations and took steps that gave them freedom. In that world, Henry Ford dreamt of an affordable car and built the Model T. John F. Kennedy dreamt of humans in the moon and humans took small steps resulting in a giant leap for mankind; Dr. Martin Luther King, dreamt of a world where one would not be judged by the color of their skin but by the content of their character, and took steps to actualize this dream before his assassination; Steve Jobs dreamt of personal computers and mobile hand held devices and made them concrete realities that we now behold. The world of magical reality produces no such artifacts - dreams and hopes remain in the cloud and never materialize. Many Africans live in this alternate world of magical reality. Thoughts of magical reality cannot be totally eliminated, but people can be reoriented to the world of concrete reality. Magical reality may be appealing, but it is a world of fantasy, an escape from reality that does not improve lives. Only those who understand the difference can transform lives.

Opening African minds

In order to achieve success in setting and meeting development objectives, Africa's people must overcome the destructive mental conditioning that has stifled progress for so long. They must strive to transform some of their traditional social attitudes, and combat the chronic ignorance that results from inadequate preparation during the early schooling years. As described in part one, the burdens of ethnic intolerance, superstition, and illiteracy are among black Africa's most stubborn obstacles to social and economic reform. Africans can only reverse the crippling effects of these and other negative influences by educating, focusing, and liberating their own minds from beliefs that are out of step with the modern world of technological progress and democratic, multicultural social values.

Young minds are the most receptive to learning, and universal education should provide children and young people with the necessary tools for understanding and managing the environments in which they live. Basic education in most African countries must serve the function of helping to dispel inaccurate or misleading beliefs and destructive social prejudices. By offering evidence-based explanations for distressing phenomena and demonstrating the power of multicultural collaboration, African educators can begin the process of opening young minds to the possibilities and opportunities offered by the modern world.

Naturally, as people age they become less receptive to new ideas, and it is more difficult to influence or change attitudes long embedded in existing social culture. Respect must be shown for traditions that still serve important functions in maintaining coherence of families and communities, but wherever destructive cultural beliefs and practices that impede healthy social and economic development are identified, they must be discarded. Efforts must be made to reeducate adult populations by offering advice and solutions to address entrenched barriers. Adults would benefit from public education on subjects such as women's health and prenatal care, basic techniques for safe water management, conflict resolution ethnic tolerance, and the fundamentals of business practice.

Emphasis must always be placed on social tolerance, public account-ability, and openness to new methods.

In highly developed societies, the proofs of success are more often revealed through long-term strategies that demonstrate commitment to a well-laid plan, and it is the adherence to such structured goals that compel respect and admiration. While there are always cases of individuals who strike it rich through sheer luck or fortuitous connections, the majority of people who achieve personal and professional success and improved quality of life do so by making sound decisions about education and career development, and focusing their ambitions toward personal and professional growth. The attitude required for this kind of success is characterized by determination, forward thinking, and self-confidence—rather than by a need for affirmation from others based solely on appearances or divine grace.

Embracing new technologies

Africans have tended to be conservative and somewhat hostile toward technological change, and adoption of new technologies has lagged in many areas. Of course, even in the most isolated and under-served areas, Africans appreciate the benefits offered by familiar technologies such as automotive transport, telecommunications and electrical power, though many do not have access to these amenities at even the most basic level. However, it is not only a lack of access that impedes utilization of more advanced technologies in many areas of Sub-Saharan Africa, but traditional attitudes toward the natural world are often at odds with the mindset of the science-based, technology-driven modern world. In order to increase the penetration and adoption of efficient technological solutions, outreach efforts must be mounted to demonstrate the efficacy, cost-effectiveness, and sustainability of new machines and methods that are developed to suit the environments in which they are to be deployed.

When portable the electric yam-pounding machine was first introduced to the Nigerian market in the 1980s, potential consumers were reluctant to accept the device, although it greatly eased the work involved in food preparation. Similarly, many Nigerians initially rejected the concept of frozen fish when it was first introduced, refusing to buy or eat it.

In construction sites throughout the continent, many workers still rely on manually-operated tools, such as hand-held saws, instead of motorized cutting tools and drills. This resistance to time-saving, convenient and cost-cutting alternatives can discourage potential developers and entrepreneurs from bringing valuable new products into African markets. The challenge is therefore to create solutions that fill technology gaps, while educating the public about the benefits provided.

Communications technology is one area in which Africa can leap over infrastructural hurdles that have frustrated development for years. Wireless phone and internet access can offer immediate connectivity to millions of users, and bring the benefits of twenty-first century global communication to urban and rural communities alike. This technological boon opens new avenues for financial services and e-commerce, as well as information transfer and educational outreach. Most Africans are eager to embrace this kind of technology, as it offers boundless opportunities in social, cultural, and economic activity. Therefore, high priority must be given to increasing penetration, expanding access, and lowering costs of service and related hardware.

Improving education systems

This book calls for an African age of reformation and enlightenment, similar to the eras of change that launched Western culture toward global domination. This can only be achieved through the widespread institution of progressive educational curricula that expand Africans' capacity for inquiry, exploration, and discovery, and reconnect them with their innate abilities to think freely and act creatively. These new curricula must offer better ways of understanding the forces that drive progress in the real world, and a coherent array of responses to the difficult circumstances confronting Africans today. Students should be encouraged to challenge assumptions that arise from customary practices and long-held beliefs, so they can discover appropriate solutions to problems that their ancestors never encountered.

Many Africans still understand their environment in terms of mystical beliefs, rather than immutable laws of science. They rely largely on instinct and intuition, neglecting their powers of empirical observation and rational analysis. Though finely tuned instinct is an invaluable asset in determining how to respond in challenging situations, the forces of intellectual and creative thought have driven the success of civilizations that have dominated the world stage. Education has therefore become the most important element of socialization in every modern developed nation, and this must be true in Africa as well.

In black Africa today, many government-sponsored schools have been neglected – they are without windows, doors or electricity -classrooms are overcrowded, teachers are underqualified and poorly paid, curricula are inadequate or irrelevant, and many students are unable to attend school because their families cannot afford the fees. A crucial step in lifting black Africa's burden will be the implementation of aggressive educational reform programs based on contemporary models of learning.

In order to build a society in which ambition, hard work and dedication to worthy goals are rewarded and admired, strong emphasis must be placed on the value of quality education beginning at an early age, for boys and girls alike. Children must learn self-discipline and solid academic skills, and their intellect and imagination must be engaged in the quest for greater knowledge and understanding of the issues they will need to engage later in life. Thus armed and enlightened, black Africans of the younger generations will be able to tackle the enormous challenges ahead, and create their own new beginnings. Therefore primary and secondary education should be free and mandatory. Children must be encouraged to develop inquiring and investigative minds from their earliest educational experience.

Developing vocational skills

The lack of people trained in vocational skills is an added burden to Africa's aspirations for development. According to the United Nations Educational, Scientific, and Cultural Organization (UNESCO), less than five percent of Africans enroll in formal technical or vocational training programs. Many positions for technicians, welders, mechanics, engineers, plumbers, and electricians remain open because of the number of qualified locals is low, so, Africans turn to skilled foreigners to do these jobs.

Technical vocational education and training (TVET) should be promoted as an alternative career development path offering enhanced employment opportunities. Since there is a deficit of Africans trained in vocational skills, and these services will increasingly be required as economies modernize and infrastructural development progresses. The Moroccan government has introduced an innovative approach that allows private sector partners to develop public TVET programs aimed at preparing trainees for specific jobs in important development areas, such as the automotive and aeronautics industries.[65] Describing how the private sector can be engaged in skills development, Muriel Dunbar wrote:

> To develop the supplier base for the automotive industry, the government encouraged Renault to set up a plant in Morocco and established the Institute for Training Automotive Professionals in 2011. The government provided the initial capital investment while Renault developed the curriculum and trained the faculty. The Moroccan government will subsidise operating costs until 2014; after that date, the industry will pay. The programme will train Renault's 6,000 employees until 2014; after which point it plans to expand its target to the 30,000 employees of Renault's 125 or so SME suppliers.[66]

This approach can serve as a model for black African nations seeking to promote the development of a skilled indigenous workforce, and a strong industrial base.

African greatness resides in the minds and hearts of all black Africans, and if they embrace and express the power within them, they will brighten the world with their brilliance. The shadows of the past that cloud their minds with doubt and despair must be dispersed through progressive modern education, and new opportunities for production and employment must be opened through the economical use of every available resource. With cooperation and commitment to a better life for all, the people and the nations of Sub-Saharan Africa will show the world how strong they are, and what wonders they can accomplish.

Young Africans cannot afford the malaise that characterizes the so-called millennial generations of rich, developed countries; they must understand that education is a priceless commodity, and offers the only hope for the future of African nations. Likewise, leaders and educators must see the African classroom as a laboratory for the development of their most precious resource—the ingenuity and intellectual energy of young people.

CHAPTER 10

Promoting Social Development and Stability

"I dream of an Africa which is in peace with itself."
Nelson Mandela.

Championing self-sufficiency at the local level

Developed countries can withstand periodic crises, because they have well-established social, political, and economic structures that absorb shockwaves and prevent full-scale collapse. However, most African nations have not yet developed stable institutions, let alone long-term socioeconomic sustainability. Therefore a primary aim of development policy must be to strengthen the basic elements of economic, political, and social stability at the roots of society.

Initial interventions should seek to reinforce the internal self-sufficiency of African communities, many of which are functioning at subsistence level. This goal cannot be accomplished through sweeping programs of top-to-bottom change. On the contrary, new social and economic systems must be built from the ground up and nurtured as they grow. Incremental micro-level changes can yield enormous macro-level results, with the necessary investment of time, energy, and resources.

Emphasizing the benefits of community effort

Community projects offer an ideal means for solving pressing local problems, and revitalizing urban neighborhoods and rural settlements alike. Cooperative efforts can increase self-sufficiency by expanding access to essential resources, improving local infrastructure, and providing support for those in need. In most traditional African societies, the good of the group supersedes that of the individual. Members of any social unit are expected to serve the interests of the community and contribute to its material and spiritual well-being. However, the influence of social customs transferred during the colonial and industrial eras has diluted this aspect of African tradition, and a spirit of individualism is now more widely accepted, often to the detriment of community life.

Groups that are not united by common aims and principles can never cohere, and they lose the problem-solving advantage that is gained whenever people engage in a cooperative effort. Reviving the traditional African spirit of community activism will, therefore, be a key to addressing many basic needs at the local level, particularly in isolated rural areas than by individual efforts or outside intervention. When the creative and productive potential of community members is mobilized toward a common goal, greater and longer-lasting progress can be achieved.

Africans living in both urban and rural areas should identify local development projects that can be undertaken as community efforts, using volunteer labor and other in-kind contributions. Such projects could include constructing water storage facilities or drainage systems, building simple wooden bridges and walkways, clearing and stabilizing access roads, or simply setting a specific day aside each month for cleaning up the neighborhood. Rather than waiting for aid to be provided by state agencies or international NGOs, Africans should seize the initiative to improve local conditions. This can eliminate months or years of stagnation and missed opportunities, and raise the living standards of individuals and families throughout the communities served. Combining efforts and pooling resources of people with shared needs creates material value for everyone involved.

The role of African diaspora aid organizations

It is widely believed that Africans in the diaspora can play an essential role in development initiatives on the continent, by garnering resources available abroad and leveraging their professional credentials and experience to press the most urgent issues for reform. A large number of organizations have been established with these goals in mind, and they can serve as magnets for members of the African diaspora who are committed to creating change for the better in the land of their birth.

While many Africans living abroad support relatives and colleagues at home through regular remittance payments, diaspora aid organizations create a wider avenue for providing support to those who are striving toward a better life on African soil. Contributing through financial donations is one option, but volunteering as a consultant, teacher, or mentor can be just as valuable, and much more personally rewarding. Nothing can approach the feeling of pride and accomplishment that comes from seeing a development project through from the planning stage to completion, and observing the improvements that result in the lives of individuals and communities who benefit from such collaborative efforts.

Now is the time for educated and successful black African men and women living abroad to rise above their tribal and ideological differences and collaborate in the urgent work of constructing a brighter African future. There are numerous organizations and NGOs doing life-saving charitable work in Africa. Organizations such as Africans in the Diaspora, African Diaspora Marketplace, the Aspire Institute of Business and Technology, and numerous UN organizations aim to ensure that children born in black Africa today will enter adulthood on equal footing with their counterparts in developed nations around the world. Africans who have met the challenges of beginning life in their homeland, and have built their homes and careers in the developed world, can form a bridge of hope across the chasm that separates the worlds of their experience. Among these are people who know what needs to be done, and how best to do it.

A large number of Africans in the diaspora and at home are eager to see tangible action at the national, state, and local levels of African government to address the pressing socioeconomic issues that affect so many on the continent. But African functionaries often have limited expertise in the areas of their responsibility, and may feel little or no pressure to actualize important development initiatives. Diaspora organizations can facilitate progressive action by helping government leaders and senior bureaucrats improve performance and achieve better results in projects that raise living standards throughout black Africa. Africans in the diaspora who have professional training and experience in specific development areas can serve as valuable resources, offering relevant, easily implementable solutions.

The prodigious number of African diaspora organizations operating today is a sign of the enormous will for change that exists in diaspora communities; one online listing shows 80 separate entries in North America alone.[67] However, these groups could certainly be more effective if there were greater collaboration and cross-fertilization among them, or if they joined forces to tackle larger projects and widen their networks of potential donors and volunteers. This could also serve to increase communication among national or ethnic groups engaged in similar development activities, and could, therefore, benefit from the exchange of information and technology.

An African Progress Corps (APC)

Intra-African volunteer programs can provide assistance to communities in need, while helping participants gain insight into the culture and traditions of different ethnic or national groups. For decades, successful organizations, such as the Peace Corps and the Cross-Cultural Corps, have not only enlisted countless volunteers to serve in local communities throughout Africa, but have also acted as vehicles for promoting tolerance and understanding among members of different cultural groups.

Drawing from this model, an African Progress Corps (APC) can be established to recruit professionals in diverse fields such as education, healthcare, engineering, natural sciences, and information technology, to help promote development in African communities across the continent. APC volunteers can provide specialist assistance for sustainable community projects, guiding efforts by local groups committed to increasing their own self-reliance through positive change. The objective of the APC initiative would be to mobilize African professionals at home and abroad to apply their expertise and experience in direct, practical interventions that will improve the lives and prospects of their fellow Africans.

In partnership with NGOs operating in Africa, and in keeping with clearly defined priorities determined by national and provincial governments or local community councils, an APC regional coordinating committee would be responsible for identifying and recruiting professionals to serve in specific areas of development within a given community. Reports of projects undertaken and completed would be published annually to enable proper assessment of these programs. Further, the African Progress Corps would be:

- operated as a not-for-profit organization;
- organized and coordinated at the regional level, based on African Union regional economic zones;
- funded by individual donors, corporations and government grants.

APC volunteers would stay as guests in the host communities, to develop a deeper understanding of the issues involved in the project at hand, and strengthen their ties with the community. This experience would be culturally enriching and emotionally rewarding for those who offer their services through this program, and would expand the social horizons of the local people.

Youth services – teaching social responsibility at an early age

Nigeria and South Africa have successful National Youth Service Programs. These programs need to be strengthened and adopted across the continent, and provisions made for young people to be given the option to perform their yearly community service in any African country or region of their choice. In addition to benefiting the communities served, this could instill a sense of social commitment in young Africans, and provide valuable work experience to enhance their career potential. The stated goals of the Nigerian and South African programs are as follows:

Nigerian Youth Service Corps - Objectives[68]	South Africa Youth Service - Objectives[69]
• To inculcate discipline in Nigerian youths by instilling in them a tradition of industry at work, and of patriotic and loyal service to Nigeria in any situation they may find themselves. • To raise the moral tone of the Nigerian youths by giving them the opportunity to learn about higher ideals of national achievement, social and cultural improvement • To develop in the Nigerian youths the attitudes of mind, acquired through shared experience and suitable training. which will make them more amenable to mobilisation in the national interest • To enable Nigerian youths acquire the spirit of self-reliance by encouraging them to develop skills for self-employment • To contribute to the accelerated growth of the national economy • To develop common ties among the Nigerian youths and promote national unity and integration • To remove prejudices, eliminate ignorance and confirm at first hand the many similarities among Nigerians of all ethnic groups • To develop a sense of corporate existence and common destiny of the people of Nigeria. • The equitable distribution of members of the service corps and the effective utilisation of their skills in area of national needs • That as far as possible, youths are assigned to jobs in States other than their States of origin • That such group of youths assigned to work together is as representative of Nigeria as far as possible • That the Nigerian youths are exposed to the modes of living of the people in different parts of Nigeria	Inculcate a culture of service by supporting youth to participate constructively in nation-building; • Promote social cohesion; • Create understanding in young people of their role in promotion of civic awareness, patriotism and national reconstruction; • Develop the skills, knowledge and ability of young people to enable them to make the transition to adulthood; • Improve youth employability through opportunities for work experience, skills development and support to gain access to economic and further learning opportunities; and • Harness the nation's untapped human resource and provide a vehicle for enhancing the delivery of the country's development objectives especially to disadvantaged and underserved communities.

Nigerian Youth Service Corps - Objectives[68]	South Africa Youth Service - Objectives[69]
• That the Nigerian youths are encouraged to eschew religious intolerance by accommodating religious differences • That members of the service corps are encouraged to seek at the end of their one year national service, career employment all over Nigeria, thus promoting the free movement of labor • That employers are induced partly through their experience with members of the service corps to employ more readily and on a permanent basis, qualified Nigerians, irrespective of their States of origin	

Providing opportunities for this kind of character-building field service to young Africans in their formative years can produce results more quickly than programs designed to reeducate whole communities, where established habits and complex webs of relationships can make social change a slow and challenging process.

Strengthening social support systems

As Africa continues to urbanize and awaken to industrialization, social support systems must be strengthened to guarantee health and a safety net for society's most vulnerable members. Traditional caretaking networks are already weakening under the influence of market-based economic models and the fierce competition they breed, while the burden of sheer survival weighs heavily on those who are unable to compete, due to poorly developed skills, age, or infirmity. In order to maintain social order and avoid the creation of a permanent underclass, progressive measures must be taken to provide for citizens who are unable to provide for themselves, and especially for children who may otherwise fall prey to disease, starvation, abuse, trafficking, or other criminal activities.

Government policies can help strengthen traditional family support systems by providing for maternity and childcare services, as well as care and support for the elderly, disabled and mentally ill. As families move to cities and women increasingly obtain employment outside the home, those who traditionally were protected by extended family and community networks will fall through the cracks of modernizing social structures. Without fair and effective social support systems designed to assist those in need, too many Africans will have to focus on the daily struggle for survival, rather than striving for personal, professional and societal development. Those left without hope for the future will weigh heavily on society, and this will impede healthy growth. It must be emphasized that social support programs must avoid known pitfalls that create dependency.

One example of programs designed to support the vulnerable and poor is the Hunger Safety Net Program of Kenya,[70] which offers direct cash transfers via biometric smart cards in four counties at risk from drought and high levels of poverty. This two-phase program is administered by the Kenyan government in partnership with the United Kingdom Department for International Development (DFID) and the Australian Agency for International Development (AusAID). This kind of initiative can help people stand on their feet when circumstances beyond their control force them to their knees. However, it cannot be seen as a long-term solution to endemic poverty.

Tapping the transformative powers of art, entertainment, and sports

Exuberance, warmth, and friendliness are positive personal characteristics widely associated with black Africans, and these natural tendencies offer an inroad toward mutual cooperation and understanding. The African proclivity for socializing through music and dance can be used to bridge gaps between disparate groups, building a sense of unity for the greater good of all Africans. By enjoying opportunities to engage in a cultural exchange through natural social interactions, Africans of every nation can discover that they have more in common than they ever knew. Africa's shared goal should be to create avenues for cultural diffusion across all boundaries, through celebratory social encounters driven entirely by innate African creativity and lust for life.

Each of the hundreds of black African ethnic groups has its own distinct form of musical expression that has evolved over centuries or millennia. Though most black Africans are conservative in their taste for traditional music, and tend to prefer the familiar sounds of their own heritage, the drum-driven rhythms that characterize all African folk music elicit a primal response in black Africans, regardless of their cultural origins. Learning to appreciate the musical traditions of other African ethnic groups can create a bond of understanding much stronger than the flood of words poured out in conferences and symposia that are organized to build bridges between diverse cultures. When a Ghanaian listener thrills to the sound of a Malian singer, a deep connection opens that cannot be closed.

As African musical expression evolved under cross-cultural influences, and as new technologies have expanded opportunities for access and diffusion, audiences for every style of music on the continent have grown and diversified. "Makossa"[71] music and the associated dance called "bikutsi" originated in Cameroon, but they have since gained popularity throughout the sub-continent. Similarly, new genres of music and dance such as "Azonto" and "Alingo," are now wildly popular throughout Africa. This kind of cultural amalgamation fosters understanding and unity among diverse groups, erasing borders and strengthening bonds between Africans who may have lived within the physical and cultural boundaries of separate ethnic enclaves all their lives.

This cultural cross-fertilization is slowly showing its effects. There is growing evidence that the present generation of young Africans do not feel as limited by the traditions of their national and ethnic groups as their parents did, and are eager to experience a broad range of expressive styles. Internet access also offers millennial Africans a powerful medium for self-expression, social-networking, and information retrieval, with endless opportunities to reinterpret their traditions and forge a modern cultural awareness. Internet connectivity enables artistic collaboration, continuous communication and cross-cultural interaction, and young Africans are increasingly embracing this medium to bypass traditional restrictions of ethnic identity. This exciting, creative environment offers tremendous opportunities for cultural diffusion across regional boundaries.

There are many promising signs that cross-cultural connections are already yielding fruit in the areas of music and entertainment. One old song track recorded by Nigerian "Highlife" musician Rex Lawson was remixed by a young Nigerian artist in an Afro-pop style, and posted on the video-sharing site YouTube, where an Ethiopian version of the same track could also be found. The Ethiopian version was rendered in Pidgin English (spoken mostly in Anglophone West Africa), with additional lyrics in Ethiopian vernacular. Comedy is another medium in which cultural fusion can be found, and Nigerian and Ghanaian comedians now tour and perform throughout the West African sub-region, with Nigerians performing comedy in Accra, and Ghanaian actors featuring in Nigerian films that can be seen in every country along the Atlantic coast from Liberia to Gabon. The scale of inter-regional cooperation and interaction in the entertainment arts is expanding by leaps and bounds.

The role of arts festivals

One way to promote pan-African cultural awareness is through large-scale festivals, such as the African Festival of Arts and Culture (FESTAC[72]) held in Lagos, Nigeria in 1977. This event was widely heralded as a harbinger of African cultural unity, but it has not been repeated, due, in part, to the great expense of such a monumental venture. It was attended by 17,000 people from 50 countries, who came to enjoy music, dance, poetry, sculpture, painting, cinema, theatre, fashion, architecture, design, performances, and exhibits. This type of event could be instrumental in building momentum toward a more peacefully multicultural African society, and consideration should be given to developing a more effective model for the festival. The host nation could be determined through a bidding process driven by the incentives of infrastructural development, employment, and commercial activity, as well as positive public perception. Corporate sponsorship and donations from wealthy individuals and the government would reduce the overall expense while maintaining the positive momentum generated. Holding the festival in three or five-year cycles will also mitigate the stress associated with organizing the event and conflict with international events such as the African Cup of Nations, FIFA World Cup, and International Olympics. Smaller regional festivals are regularly produced throughout black Africa, and effort should be made to link these events through promotional outlets that can broaden the range of audience attracted to attend. Organizations such as the African Music Festival Network (AMFN), which is funded by the Danish Ministry of Foreign Affairs, should proliferate on the continent, with the support of African public/private coalitions.

While government sponsored and privately, organized events can contribute enormously to the promotion and dissemination of indigenous African culture, they cannot be expected to generate deeply personal connections that change attitudes for a lifetime. True cultural awareness is driven by social forces, through regular participation in activities that become a part of everyday life. This is one of Africa's greatest strengths, and it should remain so—music and dance define the rhythm and meaning of black African existence, from the pounding of grain for basic sustenance, to the celebrations or rituals marking the birth of a child or the death of a beloved elder. Performance is not required for art to enter the lives of black Africans, because it is a part of everything they do. All that is needed is for black Africans to open their hearts and minds, and see its bonding power.

Organized sport as a force for social and economic integration

The love of sports has increasingly been recognized as a powerful force for strengthening social ties and promoting engagement in productive enterprise, particularly in the developing world. Sports activities offer countless benefits to athletes and fans alike, and according to the UN Sport for Development and Peace International Working Group, participation in sports can promote health and disease prevention, social integration, conflict prevention or resolution, post-traumatic relief, peace building, and economic development, among other benefits.[73]

The international Olympic Games offer the best example of the unifying power of sporting events. The Olympic Movement was created to build a peaceful and better world by educating young people through sport practiced without discrimination, in a spirit of friendship, solidarity, and fair play. Some of the major activities that define the Olympic Movement include:

- Promoting sport and competitions through the intermediary of national and international sports institutions worldwide.
- Cooperation with public and private organisations to place sport at the service of mankind.
- Assistance to develop "Sport for All".
- Advancement of women in sport at all levels and in all structures, with a view to achieving equality between men and women. Help in the development of sport for all.
- Opposition to all forms of commercial exploitation of sport and athletes.
- The fight against doping.
- Promoting sports ethics and fair play.
- Raising awareness of environmental problems.
- Financial and educational support for developing countries through the IOC institution Olympic Solidarity.[74]

Investment in sports education and promotion of such events should, therefore, be a priority in every African nation, with continent-wide international cooperation to sponsor intra-African events, and to build and maintain world-class competitive teams.

Africans have upheld an extraordinary level of performance in many areas of competitive sport. The continent has its own history of sporting events similar to the Olympics - the All-Africa Games-which features competition in more than 30 sports. Africans are very enthusiastic about sports in general, and soccer in particular; a soccer field is the most common form of playground found in every nation across the continent. The Africa Cup of Nations, which showcases the best players and teams in Africa, is a vibrant continental tournament of matches among competing nations, most of which have thriving national leagues. The quality of African soccer improved tremendously in the last decade of the 20th century, with countries such as South Africa, Senegal, Togo, Mali, and the Republic of Benin rising as new powers in Africa.

However, in spite of these successes, the potential of soccer and other popular sports as drivers of social change remains virtually unexplored. The focus has been limited to its value as a peaceful forum of competition, exercise, amusement, and leisure. The enormous popular appeal of soccer can also become a platform for local, regional and national development. A UK-based charity called "Football4Africa," for example, promotes social awareness and raises funds for the support of African children.[75] Various other non-governmental organizations and the United Nations have also used sports as a tool for economic and social development, conflict resolution and fundraising for humanitarian projects. African governments, NGOs and entrepreneurs should likewise initiate campaigns that leverage the positive power of sports to build partnerships, promote business, raise funds, encourage community service, and strengthen social ties.

Sports-based initiatives must be tailored to specific social and cultural contexts, and those who initiate and manage the programs should recognize the value of maximum inclusiveness. Events should be designed to encourage widespread participation and enjoyment, in an atmosphere of peaceful enthusiasm. The UN office for Sport for Development and Peace International Working Group suggests that sports-based development programs should include other non-sporting events, to enhance their effectiveness. It also recommends integration of sports programs with other local, regional, and national development initiatives, and urges program administrators to engage and empower community participants by involving them in the design and implementation of programs through collaborative partnerships.[76]

Strengthening social cooperation through culinary cultural exchange

Food can also play an important role in social integration, as well as economic development throughout black Africa, since enjoying a meal is a fundamental element of shared culture. Encouraging Africans to explore the continent's rich and varied culinary traditions can build unity among disparate groups, because taste and smell are experienced on a deep sensory-emotional level. Discovering similarities in tastes and exploring exciting new cuisines can create a connected sense of affection and admiration for other cultures.

Yet although black Africans have easily adopted the culinary tastes of Westerners, Arabs and Asians, there has been little cross-pollination among African cuisines. All Africans love hot spices and peppers, but few recognize that such shared tastes unify the diets of the continent, and culinary culture has generally remained enclosed within regional enclaves. The wonderful variety of ingredients and preparation methods used in different regions therefore remains unknown to most Africans, who generally eat only the traditional foods of their own culture, and those imported from other continents.

Africans must be encouraged to explore the varied cuisines of their continent in the same spirit of openness with which they have embraced other culinary influences. Africans from different nations encounter each other most frequently at borders and transfer points, such as airports and seaports, and international sporting events. These points of contact offer excellent venues for introducing a variety of African cuisines to a wider audience. For example, airport restaurants could enrich their menus with a selection of dishes from various African countries. If customers find a particular dish appealing, this creates an opportunity not only for business expansion, but also widening cultural connections.

Solar technology

With solar technology advancing, it is hard to explain why Africa which has abundant sunshine year-round, has not made solar energy the focal point for its needs. Sub-Saharan Africa can be the world leader in generation and transmission of solar energy. African nations must seek to leapfrog energy generation technology and capacity in the way innovation in wireless phone technology miraculously solved Africa's telecommunication problems. Existing power generating technology such as hydro dams, fossil fuel generators, and nuclear are too capital intensive and expensive for African nations to invest for their energy needs. Therefore, Africa must invest in new technology that overcomes the barriers imposed by existing technology to solve it energy needs.

CHAPTER 11

Developing Infrastructure, Commerce and Technology

"States get to improve transportation infrastructure; that creates economic development, puts people back to work and, most important, enhances safety and improves local communities."

Corrine Brown.

Massive investment in infrastructure

A crucial step in lifting black Africa's burden will be the wide-scale modernization of basic infrastructure. At the top of a long list of urgent concerns are access to clean water and reliable electrical power, and effective waste management. Infrastructure development does not consist of constructing private houses with individual boreholes for water and generators for electric power. Instead power generation grids and public water systems must be expanded in every nation, as a lack of adequate supply places severe limitations on the potential for economic development and improvement of life quality. Nigeria the most populous black African country, with a population more than half that of the US, can only manage to generate electrical power equaling 5 percent of US output.[77]

Africa has also developed few regional or intercontinental highways, public transportation grids, or other basic systems to facilitate travel, transportation, and commerce. The lack of investment in infrastructure has rendered trade between African nations exceedingly difficult, not only by hampering the shipment of goods, but also restricting the movement of skilled and unskilled labor across regional boundaries.

113

The paradoxical result, one of the poorest regions of the world is the most expensive in which to do business. The cost of transporting goods between African nations is prohibitively high, and intercontinental shipping for import/export can be two to three times more expensive than in Southeast Asia, for example.[78]

In order to address these insufficiencies, black African nations must join forces to embark on a coordinated program of infrastructural development. A major component of the UN and OECD rural development agenda is the integration of private-public partnership (PPP) initiatives, and this approach has enormous potential for productive deployment in Africa. In a discussion note entitled, "New Partnerships to Implement a Post-2015 Development Agenda," published in March 2012, the UN System Task Team on the Post-2015 UN Development Agenda described this promising trend:

> There is a new movement of responsible investors rapidly expanding to include investment strategies that achieve financial return while delivering on development objectives. In the coming decades it is possible that there will be a growing number of social enterprises—micro businesses that simultaneously pursue profit and social objectives. Trends suggest an expanding opportunity space for multilateral organizations and the public sector to leverage and expand collaboration with the business community through initiatives such as specific and sustainable public-private partnerships (PPPs) and the UN Global Compact.[79]

National governments can collaborate with international investors to fund capital projects such as road and railway construction, energy development and water management, among other urgent needs.

One new vehicle for mobilizing infrastructure development projects is the Africa50 Fund, cosponsored by 23 African nations and the African Development Bank (AFDB). Africa50 consists of two legal units: Africa50 Project Development and Africa50 Project Finance.[80] Each unit is capitalized distinctly with its own governance structure. According to the President of the African Development Bank, Donald Kaberuka:

> Africa50 is the result of experience and innovation. The vehicle aims at mobilizing private financing to accelerate

the speed of infrastructure delivery in Africa, thereby creating a new platform for Africa's growth. Africa50 will
focus on high-impact national and regional projects in
the energy, transport, ICT and water sectors.
Africa50 is to be structured as a developmentally-oriented
yet commercially operated entity. It will be complemen-
tary to and legally independent of existing development
finance bodies in Africa. Accordingly, the operational
decisions will be made by a management team selected
solely on technical merit and demonstrated managerial
competence.[81]

This kind of public-private investment initiative is precisely what Africa
needs to jump-start development of regional, national, and international
infrastructure on the continent. Such projects will create profit for
investors, jobs for local residents, and income for local businesses and
suppliers, and the resulting improvements will boost quality of life and
economic potential for the regions served.

Increasing food production – a matter of life and death

Although a majority of black Africans are employed in food production, the sector remains grossly underdeveloped, and most countries
in the region are net food importers. Furthermore, most farms are operated at a subsistence level, without the benefit of modern equipment or
techniques, and only a fraction of arable land is under cultivation. Self-
sufficiency must be increased at every level to ensure food security in the
long term, and agricultural development will offer opportunities for economic expansion, while alleviating the heavy burden imposed by the
high price of imported foods.

Production and marketing of food is a crucial element of local
economies, providing sustenance and employment on a limited scale. In
order to address the need for increased volume and efficiency of food
production on small farms, the following initiatives can be introduced:

- Provide basic agricultural education for local farmers on subjects
  such as diversification and rotation of food crops; fertilizer use;
  water management and irrigation; and simple technological

upgrades that can be implemented using readily available materials.

- Revive local farming cooperatives and farmers markets, or encourage the formation of new ones to take advantage of economies of scale in the purchase of seed, fertilizer and other essential supplies, and to pool resources for harvesting and transportation.
- Offer seed and fertilizer subsidies and crop-failure relief for farmers who provide essential food crops to large local communities.

These simple measures could improve the lot of millions who produce their own food or depend on local sources for affordable grain products, vegetables, dairy, and meat. Since many Africans spend half their income or more on food, cost reduction and increased efficiency in food production can significantly improve quality of life for some of the world's poorest people.

The foods and preparation methods traditionally used across the continent share many similarities, and most Africans have diets consisting of locally produced grains, vegetables, fruits, milk, and meat products, as well as fresh and smoked fish. Semi-solid foods derived from root crops, such as yams or cassava, are staples throughout West and Central Africa, for example, along the Atlantic coast, the starchy paste made from fermented cassava roots traditionally accompanies soup or stew. Since many foods are widely used over large geographical areas, organizing larger-scale production for expanded marketing can cut costs, while increasing food supply. While there is currently inadequate infrastructural support for wide-scale agribusiness development, this area of production should be explored for its future potential as continent-wide development progresses.

Boosting trade and commerce

Intra-continental trade can be a potent driver of economic development and poverty reduction in black Africa. Over the years, African leaders have issued endless statements about the importance of promoting trade and commerce among African nations, but the dream of a flourishing commercial network has remained elusive, and the volume of trade among African nations is still marginal compared with other continents. In 2011, intra-continental commerce stood at just 10 percent of all African trade, as compared with rates of 70 percent for the European Union, 52 percent for Asia, 50 percent for North America, and 26 percent for South America.[82]

Black African producers primarily sell commodities such as oil, minerals, and agricultural products to source industries on other continents. Meanwhile, low rates of industrial and manufacturing activity sideline Africa as a potential marketplace for its own raw materials. Market fragmentation and high production costs present obstacles to manufacturing, and thus limit Africa's ability to participate in global value chains, in which intermediate products play an essential role.[83] Access to these global markets could encourage local specialization in production of goods and services to meet the specific needs of international partners.

Building integrated intra-continental markets will be an essential prerequisite for developing global competitiveness, and the benefits they provide in Asia, North America and Europe have already been seen. With a population of approximately one billion which is still growing strong, Africa can potentially offer a huge and diverse marketplace for its own new products. Increasing the volume of trade among African nations would raise national revenues along with commercial and personal incomes, thus strengthening African economies to compete in global markets, and lifting more Africans out of poverty and into a middle-class lifestyle.

African leaders and governments must cooperate to expand existing regional trade alliances and build commercial networks across national boundaries to rectify the current fragmentation of internal markets. This will require issues, such as high tariffs and transaction costs, be addressed through negotiation, legislation, and strict enforcement. It will also depend on the concurrent development of local, regional and continental infrastructure to enhance communication, travel, and transportation of raw materials and processed goods.

The UNCTAD Economic Development in Africa Report 2013 outlines some of the reasons for Africa's failure to expand intra-continental trade, as overemphasis on the elimination of trade barriers, and lack of focus on the development of production capacity, infrastructure, and public/private partnerships. The report calls for the design and implementation of new policies based on "developmental regionalism,"[84] which is viewed as, a more realistic approach to integration. The scope of the agenda was outlined as follows:

> The agenda extends beyond tariffs and non-tariff measures, import and export quotas and bans, technical and phytosanitary standards, to include issues such as competition policy, the provision of infrastructure and other public goods, investment, promotion of research and development and building the domestic productive capacities of both the private sector and State-owned enterprises, among other things. To ensure the greatest impact and efficiency, these policies should be harmonized and coordinated among participating countries in a regional arrangement.[85]

This model offers a more organic and dynamic approach to the complex challenges of integrating and increasing trade among African nations, which will be key to economic development and improved standard of living.

African entrepreneurs and venture capitalists

The 2013 UNCTAD economic development report also emphasizes the need for support and development of entrepreneurial small and medium-sized enterprises (SMEs), as well as larger commercial and financial ventures. Simplifying procedures for business establishment and enforcing fulfillment of the related requirements is only part of the solution, as outreach efforts will also be needed to inform potential entrepreneurs about the processes involved, to facilitate successful start-ups. As the report describes:

> African Governments should facilitate the upward mobility of enterprises and promote the growth of firms by increasing investment in training and education programmes for entrepreneurs and providing better access to finance and business services, particularly for SMEs.[86]

Furthermore, SMEs must to communicate and network with larger companies so they can learn about specific supply requirements, and adjust production accordingly. This will help develop supply chains for goods made in Africa, by Africans, using African materials, which can be sold both globally and in African markets.

Venture capitalists and other private equity investors will also have an important role in this development process, as they can provide capital to fund new businesses. A handful of African tycoons, such as Nigeria's Alhaji Aliko Dangote and Tony Elumelu, have built large financial organizations and invested heavily in African businesses, but they are exceptional cases, as most investors are still wary of the risks involved in establishing new ventures in Africa's emerging economies.

Mr. Elumelu coined the term "Africapitalism"[87] to describe the potentially transformative role of the African private sector in promoting development on the continent. He believes in the power of public-private partnership to stabilize the foundations of African economies, so they can begin to function as self-sustaining drivers of wealth creation and social support. In an interview published in "The Africa Report," Mr. Elumelu emphasized the importance of commercial investment in promoting African development:

> All this aid money that we pump into Africa has not achieved anything. If we were to use even half this money to guarantee loans to SMEs, we would see a change. The mentality should be that if we invest in 1,000 companies, 30% might fail, but we would be left with 700 decent companies. But if you push that risk to the banks they will not do it, they are not philanthropic organisations. They know that if they lend to the sector they will lose money.[88]

This development model requires patience, commitment and faith in the promise of an African future in which Africans are the main players, rather than passive followers of policies devised abroad.

Promoting industrialization

In accordance with the goals outlined in the African Union's *Action Plan for the Accelerated Industrial Development of Africa* (AIDA), African nations must prepare for large-scale industrialization if they want to profit from the added value created by processing raw materials into refined products, rather than selling them at low cost to foreign concerns. As the AIDA plan describes:

> Industrialization is a critical engine of economic growth
> and development. Indeed, industrialization is the essence
> of development. That Africa remains the poorest region
> of the world, where 34 of the 50 least developed coun-
> tries are located and in which poverty is on the increase,
> is a reflection of its low level of industrialization and
> marginalisation in global manufacturing.[89]

The AIDA plan proposes specific actions to facilitate industrial development in Africa, which includes steps to be taken at the regional, national, and international levels of African government and policy-making.[90] It offers a useful roadmap for overall development, since the prerequisites for building a strong industrial base include political and financial reforms, as well as investments in infrastructure and the development of a well-qualified workforce. The measures described in this plan should be implemented throughout black Africa with maximal cooperation among nations and within regions, to facilitate an expedited transition to a more industrial economy.

A series of reports by the Conference of Finance Ministers from the African Union and the UN Economic Commission for Africa,[91] between 2007 and 2016, emphasized the need for African nations to take control of industrial development initiatives essential to their economic survival, to ensure African interests remain at the fore. In the words of Kandeh K. Yumkella, Director-General of the UN Industrial Development Organization (UNIDO), "Industrialization does not occur by chance. It requires deliberate, persistent and consistent public-private partnerships and visionary leadership."[92] If Africans can seize the opportunity to lay the foundations of its own industrial revolution, Africa will finally become the primary beneficiaries of its own labor, and its abundant resources.

Employing Africa's labor force

Black Africa's greatest strength lies in its human capital with 54 independent nations that are home to approximately one billion citizens, and a population growth rate that is higher than any other continent. After Asia, black Africa is the most inhabited continent on earth, and there are millions of Africans in the diaspora dispersed around the globe. The sheer volume of the black African workforce represents an underdeveloped asset, and lacking adequate management and investment, this enormous human potential will largely go to waste.

In November 2012, Chairman and Chief Executive Director of the Dangote Group Alhaji Aliko Dangote disclosed that out of 13,000 applicants for 100 truck-driver jobs in his company, more than 9,000 candidates held advanced degrees, including bachelors, masters, and doctorate degrees.[93] This demonstrates two fundamental challenges that many African economies must address—high unemployment and a lack of quality jobs for highly qualified candidates. A top priority for all African governments must be the creation of attractive business environments in which small, mid-sized, large and multinational companies can flourish and provide ample employment opportunities at every level of the organization.

Since a significant and growing percentage of Africa's employable population is below the age of 25, targeting youth unemployment is a matter of great urgency. Though many governments sponsor programs to address this issue, lack of coordination and effective data gathering hampers their ability to achieve job placements for qualified youth. A report from the African Economic Outlook notes that the problem must be broached on multiple fronts simultaneously, preferably through public-private partnerships:

> Programmes to promote youth employment can be most effective when addressing all important constraints, not just one. Evaluation shows that programmes based on a single initiative are unlikely to work for the unemployed young. Instead, programmes are most effective when they address financial and skill gaps at the same time. Skill building and temporary employment programmes need

to be followed by job placements. Strong co-operation with the private sector to understand employers' needs and create opportunities for young people in the form of apprenticeships and internships are crucial.[94]

Investment in job creation and employment assistance for African youth will pay huge dividends in the long term, and prevent the grave socioeconomic ills that result when whole generations are denied opportunities for personal and professional growth.

Offering the prospect of career advancement and job stability encourages young black Africans to continue their education and remain on the continent after they achieve advanced qualifications. This is a crucial step in establishing a qualified, reliable, self-confident African workforce that will carry black Africa forward into a brighter future.

Building scientific communities

If black Africa hopes to make substantial, lasting contributions to the technological advancement of the human race in the new millennium, African nations must foster a culture of scientific inquiry and innovation. Priority should be given to strengthening university programs in the hard sciences, and retaining successful graduates as professors and research scientists, rather than watching them disappear to more attractive positions abroad. Many of Africa's problems require innovative technological solutions, and African scientists should be the best qualified to develop home-grown technologies designed to fit the precise specifications of the environment in which they will be deployed. The startup landscape and the emergence of technological hubs in Africa is an encouraging sign. Kenya, Nigeria, Ghana, South Africa, and Rwanda are fast becoming centers for technological innovation. It is estimated that 200 technology hubs have emerged in the last decade, including, CCHub in Nigeria, Hivecolab in Uganda, Meltwater in Ghana, Silicon Cape Initiative, JoziHub, Innovation Hub, and MLab Southern Africa in South Africa."[95]

In major African urban and cultural centers, scientific institutes should be established through public and private collaborative partnerships, to serve as hives of cross-pollination for researchers and developers in every branch of scientific inquiry. These institutions would not only offer career opportunities for African scientists on the continent, but also draw highly qualified expatriate Africans to return from the diaspora, bringing the benefits of their talent, knowledge and experience back to their homelands where they can do the most good.

African scientific centers of education and research can also lead the way toward a new era of technological advancement that will serve communities at home and abroad, and propel the development of new high-end products for global export. Africa must not remain an importer and end-user of solutions produced elsewhere. Instead, African creativity should drive the invention of innovative technologies inspired by African needs, but adaptable to the needs of emerging nations around the world.

The role of foreign investment

Though external investment and assistance will doubtless remain crucial for African development in the near and midterm, the only hope for lasting renewal and advancement will reside in energetic, unified efforts by all black Africans to reconstruct dysfunctional systems in a manner commensurate with equal opportunity in the 21st century global community. Visionary leadership and cooperation between African nations will be essential for success, as well as inter-organizational coordination of goals and efforts.

Claiming a place of respect in the eyes of the world will transform the self-image of all black Africans, and black people everywhere who suffer stigmatization and oppression because of their roots in failed ex-colonies, or in a diaspora based on centuries of human trafficking. But this transformation must also be rooted in a renaissance of organic social culture, from which black Africans have always drawn their strength. Shaking off the burdens of the past, Africans must rise together, or fall one by one.

For all black Africans, the way forward lies in coming to terms with the experiences and influences of the past, and building robust new frameworks for modern societies grounded in the unique and enduring strengths of the African people. This process will facilitate black Africa's integration into the global community of developed nations, while preserving its cultural heritage.

CHAPTER 12

Transformative leadership

"I have been impressed with the urgency of doing. Knowing is not enough; we must apply. Being willing is not enough; we must do."
Leonardo DaVinci

As described in Chapter 5, most African leaders have gravitated toward dictatorial models of government since independence was gained from the colonial powers. In order to reverse this trend, Africans must work to create a fundamental shift in popular concepts of leadership and followership. Those who choose and are chosen to lead must remain firmly oriented toward positive change and focused on building a brighter future. Furthermore, they must continually seek ways to give expression to the hopes and aspirations of their followers.[96] Africans should embrace models of leadership that build relationships based on mutual respect between the leader and the led, recognizing their fundamental interdependence.

Africa needs dedicated, visionary leaders who can find a balance between public expectations and realistic objectives based on available resources, and who can bring the citizenry along as active partners in achieving development goals. As Professor Michael Useem, Director of the Center for Leadership and Change Management at the Wharton School, University of Pennsylvania, wrote in his book *The Leadership Moment: Nine true stories of triumph and disaster and their lessons for us all.* "If ordinary people share a vision, they can take on an incredible challenge and do things they never dreamed possible."[97] Africa's burdens are shared among her people, and therefore only a shared vision

124

of a prosperous future can raise the hopes of the continent, through collaborative efforts by all those whose futures depend on the success of their urgent work.

One strategy for creating a shared vision between leaders and followers is to structure leadership relations on traditional models of African communal consensus. The advantage of this approach lies in the use of existing social systems to mobilize members of the community. It can nurture innate leadership potential at the local level, and build personal investment in decision-making and follow through. Participatory leadership ensures transparency and accountability, as all participants have access to the processes involved, and will hold each other personally accountable for the roles or tasks undertaken. Collaborative models can offer new perspectives and possibilities for leadership systems in government, business, and social organizations of every kind.

Africa will never ascend by reassembling fragments of foreign models, but also cannot be reconstructed based on traditional models that do not reflect changes that have occurred in African societies. Africa must embrace and incorporate the unique strengths of its ancient cultures into a vision for the future.

The need for strong democratic leadership

While many black African nations are represented in international media as underdeveloped, war-torn, and poverty-stricken, it is also true that over the past three decades many of their economies have experienced a surge in trade, evidenced by rapidly increasing GDP. Unfortunately, the profits of increased production and sales rarely trickle down through all levels of society to improve the general standard of living, so there is a widening rift between the few very rich and the many very poor. Corruption and mismanagement in the corridors of power divert profits of industry and charitable relief to line the pockets of the wealthy and powerful, while a majority of the people, inured to a life of poverty and exploitation, feels powerless to resist.

Leaders in government, business and professional fields must initiate policy change, establish accountability, and provide operational transparency in order to set the stage for African renewal. With the expansion of democratic principles and processes throughout the continent, black people will feel their power to help choose their nation's paths, and hold leaders accountable for promises made. Black Africans have suffered long and fought hard for the freedom of self-governance, and the future of their societies now lies in their own hands.

Promoting good governance and political stability

Since the European colonial governors ceded control of the Sub-Saharan countries, each new administration has come to power with the promise to transform their nations into a socioeconomic utopia. The mantra has always been the same—the visionary policies of the new leaders will create wealth and jobs, while providing quality education, infrastructural development, reliable utilities, general security, and so forth. Of course, the current state of most black African countries is a far cry from such lofty promises of stability and abundance. If these nations are ever to join the greater community of the developed world, their leaders must demonstrate the political will to translate exalted visions of development into concrete reality.

African leaders must ensure good governance by establishing and enforcing the rule of law, and prioritizing reforms to maximize development in the short and long term. Corruption, fraud, and mismanagement of public funds must be curtailed before any other reforms can succeed, and this will be a monumental task. Past and present leaders with proven involvement in defrauding public resources must be brought to justice, to show that this behavior will no longer be tolerated. The government is the custodian of the public wealth, and the era of siphoning public funds into personal bank accounts must be brought to a sudden close. This will require the firm establishment of accountability and transparency in the area of financial administration and cooperation by foreign governments. The citizenry must also be educated to see the benefits of holding public officials accountable.

Genuine democratization of leadership will play a crucial role in this process, as public accountability is a powerful incentive toward responsible government. If leaders must produce positive results to remain in power, they will have a vested interest in promoting the public good. The corrosive influences of nepotism and bribery must be counteracted through legislation and enforcement, as required, and free and fair elections must be ensured through rigorous oversight by objective and disinterested observers. These measures represent the minimum requirement for establishing and maintaining functional progressive governance, which is a prerequisite for sustainable socioeconomic development.

CHAPTER 13

The Role of the Church

"When the missionaries came to Africa they had the Bible and we had the land. They said 'Let us pray.' We closed our eyes. When we opened them we had the Bible and they had the land."

Desmond Tutu.

In the 1950s and 1960s, the need to sensitize the world to the scale of human suffering and mobilize Christians to take control of their liberty and lives triggered the rise of liberation theology.[98] The emergence of liberation theology represented attempts to move theology from the abstract to the real world, and call attention to the social implications of the gospel. Liberation theology emerged to deliver millions of people trapped in abstract thoughts and redirect their minds to the reality of this world. It also provided a balance between the longing of the oppressed for liberation and ecclesiastical expositions regarding spirituality.

Subsequently, liberation theology led to the rise of strong popular movements seeking profound changes in the socioeconomic structures, which contributed to poverty in many developing countries. Black liberation theology emerged from a similar quest to address issues of daily life. Quoting from scripture, Dr. Reverend Martin Luther King, Jr.[99] cautioned Americans against conforming to the world, but instead, to be transformed by renewing their minds. Dr. King's admonition shows that true Christian faith is transformational, liberating believers from the psychology of dependence on providence for solutions to human problems. Transformational religious expositions arouse the consciousness that man can transform himself by gaining control of his liberty, allowing

128

Christians to see the testimony of Christ as the ultimate gift of freedom and salvation.

Theology of productivity

In a continent where roughly a third of the population live below the poverty line and half the population remain unemployed, advancing a productive work ethic, which has stayed essentially rudimentary, is imperative for Africa's economic advancement. Increasing the share of productive capital is the surest way to change the fortunes of black Africans and the share of wealth for African nations.

The church played a role in harmonizing the gospel with the human desire for freedom; therefore, the church must play a role in providing ecclesiastical support for the message of productivity in Africa. A theology of productivity focuses attention on the problems of this world and the search for solutions[100]. Similar to liberation theology, a theology of productivity is concerned with the economic aspects of salvation not just in spiritual terms, but also in physical terms. It seeks to address concrete circumstances, rather than abstract concerns.

The book of Genesis in the Bible explicitly states that God created human beings in his own image and likeness, indicating that humans possess creative and cognitive capabilities to determine right from wrong. This view of Christianity provides the deepest meaning and complete fulfillment of the human quest to harmonize their spiritual and material needs. Theology of productivity stems from the Christian understanding that humans are created in God's image, and that they are endowed with godlike qualities, that must be used to transform themselves and the environment.

A theology of productivity allows humans to perceive God as the chief architect of production, the grand master of creativity who made the earth and the universe through the process of creation. This understanding of the gospel not only provides support for balancing human spiritual and material needs, it is also liberating and empowering.

As black Africans struggle to overcome the burden of underdevelopment, they should be cautious about religious sermons that sedate or propagate ideas that have little or no basis in reality. Credulous followership must give way to a deliberate effort to shape black

Africa's physical landscape and future. An understanding of this concept of the gospel is central to breaking free from the shackles of superstition, and tapping to the God-given ability to create and transform the environment. Africans must go to work to overcome their burdens, recognizing that the African, as a human being, is a complex, intelligent, creative, and masterfully sculptured agent in God's image.

CHAPTER 14

Success stories –
African models of good governance

"Sustainable development is the pathway to the future we want for all. It offers a framework to generate economic growth, achieve social justice, exercise environmental stewardship and strengthen governance."

Ban Ki-moon.

During the past decade, economic and social progress has been achieved in some African nations, and real growth can be seen across the continent. These changes are widely heralded as signs of an upward trend toward a long-awaited African renaissance. It is important to recognize the accomplishments of nations that have successfully restructured dysfunctional systems to ensure their progress is solidly rooted in firm ground, so development can continue, uninterrupted by the natural and economic shocks that afflict every society. However, there are only a handful of African nations that are actually achieving this goal. They should serve as examples of good governance and sound economic policy for all black African nations struggling to relieve the many burdens afflicting their people.

Ghana

Ghana has emerged as a black African nation rising from the ashes the post-colonial malaise, and has received positive assessment for its effort. The World Bank's Country Overview for Ghana, notes the nation's "stable and mature democracy," is built on its "strong multi-party political system, growing media pluralism and strong civil society activism."[101] The report goes on to describe Ghana's commendable development in the area of press freedom, and its above-average ranking in the Worldwide Governance Indicators, adding:

> This performance reflects the positive effects of an improving environment for democratic governance, coupled with a gradual improvement in the effectiveness of public institutions and persistent economic growth, resulting in Ghana attaining a lower middle income status.[102]

Ghana's development record demonstrates how political stability drives economic performance, and how democratic process and social cohesion contribute to this positive, productive dynamic.

Cape Verde

In 2011, the prestigious and valuable Ibrahim Prize for Achievement in African Leadership was awarded for the first time in three years, and the recipient was Pedro Veronia Pires, former President of the Cape Verde Islands. In presenting this award, the Mo Ibrahim Foundation recognized President Pires' role in transforming his country for the better. The Salim Ahmed Salim, Chair of the award committee noted:

> Under his ten years as President, the nation became only the second African country to graduate from the United Nation's Least Developed category and has won international recognition for its record on human rights and good governance..[103]

The result is that Cape Verde is now seen as an African success story, economically, socially and politically. Cape Verde's success story is also reflected in the World Bank's Country Overview, which likewise commends the nation's success in establishing and maintaining a stable and highly democratic political process. The economic consequences of this achievement are duly noted:

> In December 2007, Cape Verde achieved middle-income country status. Good governance, sound macroeconomic

management, including strong fiscal discipline and credible monetary and exchange-rate policies, trade openness and increasing integration into the global economy, a responsible use of donor support, and the adoption of effective social development policies have produced impressive results throughout the Cape Verdean archipelago.[104]

Here again, we see the power of good governance in fostering sustainable free-market economic development, which can never be attained under political conditions of instability, chaos or oppressive control.

Botswana

When Botswana achieved independence in 1966, it was one of the poorest countries in Africa and the world, sparsely populated, with no proven resources. Shortly thereafter, the discovery of large diamond deposits offered a way out of this destitution, and a productive partnership was formed with South African diamond company De Beers, with each partner holding a 50 percent interest. Since then, Botswana has blossomed into one of Africa's most successful nations, praised for its stable representative government and its wise management of valuable natural resources. In an assessment of how far this country has come, Jane Williams wrote for the prestigious INSEAD international school of business:

Through good governance and prudent macroeconomic and fiscal management, Botswana has escaped the "resource curse" afflicting many of its resource-rich neighbours still struggling with poverty, corruption, civil war and under-development...

The country's insistence on the highest degree of transparency, its zero corruption tolerance and the creation of an independent judiciary which "governs the governors" ranks it consistently among the highest in Transparency International's corruption perceptions index.[105]

This assessment is corroborated by the World Bank's Country Overview, which states, "the country has a mature democracy, with free and fair elections held regularly and the constitution provides for fundamental rights and freedoms."[106] However, the report also enumerates various concerns that could affect future development, including relatively high rates of severe poverty, the spread of HIV/AIDS, and a strong dependence on the diamond industry, which is not expected to continue producing at a high capacity in the long term. Botswana must concentrate on diversifying its economy over the next decade, if it hopes to maintain its status as one of Africa's greatest success stories.

Mauritius

Since the island realm of Mauritius gained independence from Great Britain in 1968, it has been transformed into one of the most stable nations in black Africa, with a diverse middle-income economy and well-established democratic institutions. It holds top ranking among African nations in various indices measuring good governance, competitiveness and favorability of investment climate. Some of the measures implemented to ensure continued development are described in the World Bank's Country Overview:

> Since 2010, the government embarked on a second generation reform program to continue improving Mauritius' competitiveness as it transitions to more diversified export markets, while ensuring that growth remains socially inclusive. Key elements of this reform are the improvement of: (i) the delivery of public services, including the civil service and public enterprises; (ii) the development of infrastructure to overcome critical bottlenecks, particularly in transportation; (iii) the development of skills to enhance productivity and better integrate those parts of the population that lag behind; (iv) social protection to provide empowerment opportunities to the more vulnerable population; and (v) the further liberalization of non-tariff measures to improve trade competitiveness.[107]

This outline could serve as a model for any African nation seeking to enhance its development potential, strengthen and improve governmental and social structures, and increase opportunities for participation in the global economy.

The political and economic achievements of Mauritius would be noteworthy for any developing country, but particularly for a newly independent black African island nation with no natural resources of its own. In a digest written for the private United States-based National Bureau of Economic Research, Laurent Belsie describes what can be learned by studying the Mauritian example:

> The island's accomplishments suggest at least three possible lessons for the rest of Africa. First, trade is crucial to growth. Second, ethnic differences can be accommodated by a well-designed parliamentary political system. Third, democracies can reform economic systems in ways that foster economic growth.[108]

Though conditions differ across the continent and complex challenges abound in every corner of black Africa, with careful planning and perseverance, each nation can find its own way toward a better life for its people, a fuller partnership with its neighbors, and a place in the developed world—with all the rights and benefits that this confers.

Epilogue

Still I Rise
You may write me down in history
With your bitter, twisted lies,
You may tread me in the very dirt
But still, like dust, I'll rise.

Does my sassiness upset you?
Why are you beset with gloom?
'Cause I walk like I've got oil wells
Pumping in my living room.

Just like moons and like suns,
With the certainty of tides,
Just like hopes springing high,
Still I'll rise.

Did you want to see me broken?
Bowed head and lowered eyes?
Shoulders falling down like teardrops.
Weakened by my soulful cries.

Does my haughtiness offend you?
Don't you take it awful hard
'Cause I laugh like I've got gold mines
Diggin' in my own back yard.

You may shoot me with your words,
You may cut me with your eyes,
You may kill me with your hatefulness,
But still, like air, I'll rise.

Does my sexiness upset you?
Does it come as a surprise
That I dance like I've got diamonds
At the meeting of my thighs?

Out of the huts of history's shame
I rise
Up from a past that's rooted in pain
I rise
I'm a black ocean, leaping and wide,
Welling and swelling I bear in the tide.
Leaving behind nights of terror and fear
I rise
Into a daybreak that's wondrously clear
I rise
Bringing the gifts that my ancestors gave,
I am the dream and the hope of the slave.
I rise
I rise
I rise.
Maya Angelou

Notes and References

Preface

Friedman TL. *The world is flat: A brief history of the twenty-first century.* New York: Farrar, Straus and Giroux; 2005.

Introduction

World energy outlook. International Energy Agency (IEA). UNESCO Website. Unesco.org Accessed August 26, 2016.

The World Factbook (CIA). https://www.cia.gov/library/publications/the-world-factbook/rankorder/ 2232rank. html Accessed August 26, 2016.

Chapter 1 – The Black Burden

1. Chronological list of African independence. About Education. http://africanhistory. about.com/library/timelines/blIndependenceTime.htm Accessed August 26, 2016.

2. Nkrumah K. *Neo-colonialism. The last stage of imperialism.* First Published: in 1965 by Thomas Nelson & Sons, Ltd., London. Published in the USA by International Publishers Co., Inc. https://politicalanthro.files.wordpress.com/2010/08/ nkrumah.pdf Accessed May 26, 2016.

3. Bortolot AI. Trade relations among European and African nations. In: Heilbrunn Timeline of Art History. 2003. New York: The Metropolitan Museum of Art Website. http://www.metmuseum.org/toah/hd/aftr/hd_aftr.htm Accessed September 1, 2016.

4. Colonization. In: Encyclopedia Britannica. https://www.britannica.com/place/ western-Africa/Colonization Accessed October 28, 2016.

5. Mutere M. African culture and aesthetics, for Kennedy Center's African Odyssey Interactive: http://artsedge.kennedy-center.org/aoi/history/ao-guide.html Accessed January 14, 2014.

6. Lassiter JE. African culture and personality: Bad social science, effective social activism, or a call to reinvent ethnology? 3(2): 1. 1999. http://web.africa.ufl.edu/asq/v3/v3i2a1.htm Accessed January 20, 2014.

Chapter 2 – Black African Phenomenology

7. Whetstone JT. Personalism and moral leadership: The servant leader with a transforming vision. *Business Ethics: A European Review.* 2002, 11(4): 385-392.

Chapter 3 – Superstition and Perceptions of the Natural World

8. Ondo police rescue 4 year old girl caged by parents for 'witchcraft.' Saharareporters Website. HTTP://SAHARAREPORTERS.COM/2016/08/25/ONDO-POLICE-RESCUE-4-YEAR-OLD-GIRL-CAGED-PARENTS-%E2%80%98WITCHCRAFT %E2% 80%99 Published August 25, 2016. Accessed August 26, 2016

9. Bures F. A mind dismembered. In search of the magical penis thieves. *Harpers Magazine.* 2008. http://harpers.org/archive/2008/06/a-mind-dismembered/

10. Ogula D. The case for a theology of productivity in Africa. Nigeria.com Website. http://nigeriaworld.com/articles/2013/nov/172.html Published November 17, 2013.

11. Ibid.

12. Ibid.

13. Ibid.

14. Ibid.

15. Ibid.

16. Nigerian Pastor Oyedepo assaults teenager in Church. Sahara TV. 2011. https://www.youtube.com/watch?v=jvKRjETbIRg Posted December 29, 2011. Accessed October 26, 2016.

17. Oluwapelumi O. "I slapped her and she came to beg!" – Is Bishop Oyedepo bragging about the 'witch slap'? Blog post. December, 2011. http://ynaija.com/i-slapped-her-and-she-came-to-beg-bishop-oyedepo-brags-about-assault-incide nt/ Accessed December 2, 2016.

18. Collins JC, Porras JI. *Clock Building not time telling.* In: Business leadership, ed. *Jossey-Bass reader.* San Francisco: Jossey-Bass Inc; 2003:399.

Chapter 4 – Education and Illiteracy in Black Africa

19. Adult and youth literacy, UNESCO Institute of Statistics 2015, p. 1-2. http://www.uis.unesco.org/literacy/Documents/fs32-2015-literacy.pdf Accessed October 14, 2016.

20. Ibid.

21. Adult and youth literacy. UNESCO September, 2011.
http://www.uis.unesco.org/FactSheets/Documents/FS16-2011-Literacy-EN.pdf
Accessed September 22, 2016.

22. Reaching the marginalized. Education for All Global Monitoring Report Regional
fact sheet – Sub-Saharan Africa. UNESCO, 2010.
http://www.unesco.org/new/fileadmin/MULTIMEDIA/HQ/ED/GMR/pdf/gmr
2010/gmr2010-fs-ssa.pdf Accessed November 12, 2016.

23. United Nations Universal Declaration of Human Rights. 1948. Palais de Chaillot,
Paris http://www.un.org/en/documents/udhr/ Accessed November 12, 2016.

24. Introduction to African languages. The African language program at Harvard. Website. http://alp.fas.harvard.edu/introduction-african-languages Accessed
November 15, 2016.

25. Aboki 4 Christ's common baby let's go. Youtube Video
https://www.youtube.com/watch?v=nBVCn5oCCRo Posted August 11, 2014.
Accessed May 19, 2016.

26. Sunday C. Amazing: 60-year old man attends secondary school Bomadi. *Vanguard.*
April 5, 2016. http://www.vanguardngr.com/2016/04/amazing-60-year-old-
man-attends-secondary-school-bomadi/ Accessed April 14, 2016.

27. Regional overview: Sub-Saharan Africa. Education for all Global Monitoring
Report. UNESCO. 2011: 2-4.
http://unesdoc.unesco.org/images/0019/001913/191393e.pdf Accessed
October 29, 2016.

28. Ibid.

29. Reaching the marginalized. Education for All Global Monitoring Report Regional
fact sheet – Sub-Saharan Africa. UNESCO, 2010.

30. Clinton WJ. Statement on the Observance of International Literacy Day. August 24,
1994. http://www.presidency.ucsb.edu/ws/?pid=49016 accessed September
30, 2016.

Chapter 5 – The Leadership Albatross

31. Kouzes JM & Posner BZ. *Leadership: The challenge.* 3rd ed. San Francisco: Jossey-
Bass; 2002.

32. Muhumuza R. Uganda's long-time ruler changes tune on longevity. *CNSnews.com.*
June 5, 2013. http://www.cnsnews.com/news/article/ugandas-long-time-ruler-
changes-tune-longevity Accessed November 13, 2016.

33. Bartholet J. A big man in Africa. *Newsweek.* May 13, 2001.
   http://www.newsweek.com/big-man-africa-153113 Accessed September 22,
   2016.

34. Bernault F. Magical politics in equatorial Africa. 2001.
   http://www.musicman1.net/Magicalpolitics.htm Accessed November 13,
   2016.

35. Rotberg R. Good leadership is Africa's missing ingredient. March 04, 2013. Special
   to The Globe and Mail. http://www.theglobeandmail.com/opinion/good-
   leadership-is-africas-missing-ingredient/article9234496/ Accessed November
   14, 2016.

36. Curnow R. Why is Africa poor? August 30, 2010. CNN Marketplace Desk.
   https://blog.standardbank.com/feed-item/why-africa-poor Accessed November 13, 2016. http://business.blogs.cnn.com/2010/09/30/why-is-africa-poor/

37. Murunga G. Africa must embrace educated leaders. *Sunday Independent.* August 12,
   2012. http://www.iol.co.za/sundayindependent/africa-must-embrace-edu-
   cated-leaders-1360441#.UeE1j77D_IW Accessed November 14, 2016.

38. Mills G. Why is Africa poor? *Money Web.* August 27, 2010.
   http://www.moneyweb.co.za/archive/why-is-africa-poor/?sn=2009%20Detail
   Accessed November 13, 2016.

39. List of countries in Africa. https://www.countries-ofthe-world.com/countries-of-
   africa.html Accessed December 2, 2016.

40. Kouzes JM, Posner BZ. *Leadership: The challenge.* 3rd ed. 2002: 129.

Chapter 6 – The Socioeconomic Burdens of Black Africa

41. Africa's hopeful economies. The continent's impressive growth looks likely to continue. *The Economist.* December 3, 2011.
   http://www.economist.com/node/21541008 Accessed November 13, 2016.

42. Africa's economy, poverty. *British Broadcasting Corporation (BBC) News.*
   http://news.bbc.co.uk/2/shared/spl/hi/africa/05/africa_economy/html/povert
   y.stm Accessed November 13, 2016.

43. OECD. African economic outlook 2013: Structural transformation and natural
   resources. *Human development in Africa. OECD Publishing.* 2013.
   www.africaneconomicoutlook.org/sites/default/files/content-
   pdf/AEO2015_EN.pdf Accessed October 22, 2016.

44. Kariuki JG. The future of agriculture in Africa. The Pardee Papers / No. 15. 2011.
   http://www.bu.edu/pardee/files/2011/11/15-PP.pdf Accessed November 20,
   2016.

45. Africa's hopeful economies. The continent's impressive growth looks likely to continue. *The Economist.* December 3, 2011.

46. Daniel S. Treasury looters recruited NDelta militants against us. President Muhammadu Buhari, reveals in US. *Vanguard.* September 24, 2016. http://www.vanguardngr.com/2016/09/treasury-looters-recruited-ndelta-militants-us-buhari-reveals-us/ Accessed December 17, 2016.

47. Wolfensohn JD. Remarks at the Reinventing Government Conference. 1999. http://web.worldbank.org/WBSITE/EXTERNAL/NEWS/0,,contentMDK:20020067~menuPK:34472~pagePK:34370~piPK:34424~theSitePK:4607,00.html Accessed November 12, 2016.

48. Where is the wealth of nations? World Bank, 2006. http://siteresources.worldbank.org/INTEEI/214578-1110886258964/20748034/All.pdf. Accessed September 22, 2016.

49. Oxfam: African advertising campaign is helping to dispel negative stereotypes. *The Guardian.* January 10, 2013. http://www.theguardian.com/world/2013/jan/10/oxfam-africa-aid-campaign Accessed November 13, 2016.

50. Reversing high toll of Nigerian pros abroad. *The Guardian, Nigeria.* June 16, 2015. http://guardian.ng/opinion/reversing-high-toll-of-nigerian-pros-abroad/ Accessed November 4, 2016.

51. Lyman PN. The Nigerian state and U.S. strategic interests. Panel presentation, Achebe Colloquium, Brown University. December 11, 2009. http://www.lnc-usa. org/blog/ghana-means-more-to-us-interests-than-nigeria-ambassador-princeton-n-lyman// Accessed October 5, 2016.

52. Hruby A. Why relative size doesn't matter to Nigeria's economy. *Newsweek.* September 11, 2016. http://www.newsweek.com/why-relative-size-doesnt-matter-nigerias-economy-496692?rx=us Accessed November 13, 2016.

53. Economic development and structural adjustment in Africa. Economic Development in Africa, UNCTAD Report, 2012, p. 3 & 4. http://unctad.org/en/Publications Library/aldcafrica2012_embargo_en.pdf. Accessed November 13, 2016.

54. Ibid.

55. Meredith M. *The fate of Africa, a history of fifty years of independence.* New York: Public Affairs; 2005:174.

56. Kar D, Freitas S, Moyo JM, Ndiaye GS. Illicit financial flows and the problem of net resource transfers from Africa: 1980-2009. May 29, 2013. http://www.gfintegrity.org/storage/gfip/documents/reports/AfricaNet Resources/execsummary-gfi_afdb_iffs_and_the_problem_of_net_resource_transfers_from_africa_1980-2009.pdf - Accessed November 13, 2016.

57. Ibid.

58. Ibid.

59. Crush J, Green T, Pendleton W, Campbell E, Simelane T, Tevera D, De Vletter F. Migration, remittances and development in Southern Africa. 2006. Southern African Migration Programme (SAMP). https://www.africaportal.org/dspace/articles/migration-remittances-and-development-southern-africa Accessed November 13, 2016.

Chapter 7 – Political, Social, and Cultural Schisms at Home and Abroad

60. Zoli C, Azar S, Ross S. Patterns of conduct Libyan regime support for and involvement in acts of terrorism. Report Prepared for M. Cherif Bassiouni, Chair, UNHRC Commission of Inquiry into Human Rights Violations in Libya. 2011. http://insct.syr.edu/wp-content/uploads/2012/09/Libya-Report-27-April-2011-final-with-Cover.pdf Accessed February 3, 2017

61. Akwei S. ECOWAS okays military intervention in Gambia, joint troops stationed at border. *Africa News*. http://www.africanews.com/2017/01/18/ecowas-okays-military-intervention-in-gambia-joint-troop-stationed-at-border/ Accessed January 27, 2017.

62. Hooks B. *Rock my soul: Black people and self-Esteem*. New York: Simon and Schuster; 2003:31-32.

63. WEB DuBois. *The talented tenth*. 1903. http://teachingamericanhistory.org/library/document/the-talented-tenth/ accessed October 4, 2016.

Chapter 8 – Lifting the Burden: The Way Forward

64. UN. Millennium Development Goals Report 2015, p. 14 & 21 http://www.un.org/millenniumgoals/2015_MDG_Report/pdf/MDG%202015%20rev%20(July%201).pdf Accessed September 22, 2016.

Chapter 9 – Educating Minds, Transforming Attitudes

65. African Development Bank (AfDB) and the Organization for Economic Cooperation and Development (OECD). *Morocco*. 2008. http://www.oecd.org/dev/emea/40578273.pdf Accessed November 10, 2016.

66. Dunbar M. Engaging the private sector in skills development. *Oxford Policy Management*. 2013. https://www.gov.uk/government/uploads/system/uploads/attachment_data/file/213937/engaging-private-sector-skills-development.pdf accessed January 3, 2017.

Chapter 10 – Promoting Social Development and Stability

67. The African Leadership and Progress Network. *Diaspora organizations*. http://africanprogress.net/diaspora-organizations-2/ Accessed December 2, 2016.

68. National Youth Service Corps. Nigeria.
http://www.nysc.gov.ng/about/objectives.php Accessed October 2, 2016.

69. National Youth Development Agency. South Africa.
http://www.nyda.gov.za/National-Youth-Service-Programme/Pages/default.
aspx Accessed October 2, 2016.

70. Hunger Safety Net Program of Kenya. http://hsnp.or.ke Accessed October 4, 2016.

71. Agostinelli DM. African music.
http://www.markisworld.com/African%20Music/African%20Music.htm
Accessed October 4, 2016.

72. FESTAC 77. UNESCO.
http://www.unesco.org/archives/multimedia/?s=films_details&pg=33&id=29
Accessed October 4, 2016.

73. UN. Sport for Development and Peace [UNOSDP]. 2011. 2nd international forum
on sport for peace & development.
https://www.un.org/sport/sites/www.un.org.sport/files/ckfiles/files/10-11_05_
2011_UN-IOC_FORUM_Geneva_REPORT_EN.pdf Accessed November 11,
2016.

74. International Olympic Committee. https://www.olympic.org/about-ioc-Institution
Accessed November 11, 2016.

75. Football4Africa. Using football to change lives. http://football4africa.org Accessed
November 11, 2016.

76. UN. Sport for Development and Peace [UNOSDP]. 2011.

Chapter 11- Developing Infrastructure, Commerce and Technology

77. The World Factbook (CIA). https://www.cia.gov/library/publications/the-world-
factbook Accessed August 26, 2016.

78. Rugwabiza V. Africa should trade more with Africa to secure future growth. April
12, 2012. A speech at the University of Witwatersrand in Johannesburg,
South Africa.
http://www.wto.org/english/news_e/news12_e/ddg_12apr12_e.htm Accessed
November 13, 2016.

79. UN. System Task Team on the Post-2015 UN Development Agenda. (2012). *New
partnerships to implement a post-2015 development agenda.* Background discussion note of Working Group E of the UN Task Team on the Post-2015 UN
Development Agenda. http://www.un.org/millenniumgoals/pdf/global_part-
nerships_Aug.pdf Accessed November 13, 2016.

80. Africa50. Africa50 infrastructure fund. http://www.africa50.com/ Accessed December 18, 2016.

81. Kaberuka D. Africa should focus on getting things done to mitigate investment risks. "Reducing Perceived Riskiness of Investing in Africa's Infrastructure." Panel presentation at the Bank's 49th Annual Meetings in the Rwandan capital, Kigali. May 20, 2014. http://www.afdb.org/en/news-and-events/article/africa-should-focus-on-getting-things-done-to-mitigate-investment-risks-kaberuka-13106/ Accessed November 13, 2016.

82. Rugwabiza V. Africa should trade more with Africa to secure future growth. April 12, 2012.

83. Ibid.

84. Economic development in Africa. Intra-African trade: Unlocking private sector dynamism. UNCTAD Report, 2013:4. http://unctad.org/en/PublicationsLibrary/aldcafrica2013_en.pdf Accessed November 13, 2016.

85. Ibid., p.97

86. Ibid., p.130

87. Tony Elumelu Foundation. http://tonyelumelufoundation.org/africapitalisminstitute/about-us/what-is-africapitalism/ Accessed May 26, 2016.

88. Ibid.

89. Action plan for industrial development of Africa. African Union Conference of Minister of Industry. 1st Extraordinary Session, September 24- 27, 2007: 1. http://www.unido.org/fileadmin/import/83934_ACTION_PLAN_ON_INDUSTRIALIZATION_Final.pdf Accessed October 24, 2016.

90. Ibid., p.5-9

91. Industrialization through trade. UN. Economic Commission for Africa. 2015 http://www.un.org/en/africa/osaa/pdf/pubs/2015era-uneca.pdf Accessed October 24, 2016.

92. United Nations Information Service. Industrialization should play central role in Africa's economic development. Press Release. March 26, 2013. http://www.unis.unvienna.org/unis/en/pressrels/2013/unisous182.html Accessed November 13, 2016.

93. Iroegbu S. Nigeria: PhD, MBA holders apply as truck drivers at Dangote Group. *This Day.* November, 2012. http://allafrica.com/stories/201211030409.html Accessed October 4, 2016.

94. Africa Economic outlook. Government action to promote youth employment: A poor track record. 2012. www.africaneconomicoutlook.org/en/in-depth/Youth_Employment Accessed November 11, 2016. http://www.africaneconomicoutlook.org/en/in-depth/youth_employment/government-action-promoting-youth-employment-has-a-poor-track-record/

95. Moime D. Kenya, Africa's Silicon Valley, epicentre of innovation. April 25, 2016. https://vc4a.com/blog/2016/04/25/kenya-africas-silicon-valley-epicentre-of-nnovation accessed December 16, 2016.

Chapter 12 – Transformative Leadership

96. Kouzes JM, Posner BZ. *Leadership: The challenge.* 3rd ed. 2002.

97. Useem M. *The leadership moment. Nine true stories of triumph and disaster and their lessons for us all.* New York: Random House; 1998:125-126.

Chapter 13 – The Role of the Church

98. Liberation theology. In: Encyclopedia Britannica. https://www.britannica.com/topic/liberation-theology Accessed October 18, 2016.

99. Hooks. *Rock my soul: Black people and self-Esteem.* 2003:31-32.

100. Ogula. The case for a theology of productivity in Africa. November 17, 2013.

Chapter 14 – Success Stories – African Models of Good Goverance

101. World Bank. Ghana, overview. http://www.worldbank.org/en/country/ghana/overview Accessed October 18, 2016.

102. Ibid.

103. 2011 Ibrahim Laureate - President Pedro De Verona Rodrigues Pires. Citation & Achievements. 2011. Mo Ibrahim Foundation Website. http://www.moibrahim foundation.org/laureates/#President-Pedro-de-Verona-Rodrigues-Pires Accessed October 18, 2016.

104. World Bank. Capeverde, overview. http://www.worldbank.org/en/country/capeverde/overview Accessed October 18, 2016.

105. Williams J. Diamonds, discipline and development: Botswana comes of age. Insead School of Business. February 22, 2012. http://knowledge.insead.edu/economics-politics/botswana-comes-of-age-685

106. World Bank.Botswana, overview. http://www.worldbank.org/en/country/botswana/overview Accessed October 18, 2016.

107. World Bank. Mauritius, overview. http://www.worldbank.org/en/country/mauritius/overview Accessed October 18, 2016.

108. The National Bureau of Economic Success. *Mauritius: African Success Story.* http://www.nber.org/digest/may11/w16569.html Accessed November 12, 2016

About the Author

Dr. David Ogula was born and raised in Sub-Saharan Africa. As a child, he was curious about life beyond his immediate rural surroundings and dreamt of a better and a brighter future. His pursuit of that dream propelled him to the United States, a world vastly different from his homeland, with almost limitless opportunities. The opportunity and experience of a better life in America proved that the dream of a better life is a reality human ingenuity creates. This realization strengthened his resolve to help those he left behind, especially those children who may never have the same opportunities he had. Drawing from his experience and observations on both sides of the Atlantic, David Ogula provides an introspective insider perspective about Africa's burdens. His assessment of Africa's burdens and the solutions proffered are insightful and compelling. Join Dr. Ogula on this journey to chart Africa's future.

Dr. Ogula lives with his wife and children in Long Island, New York. He is devoted most of his time in the United States to mobilizing resources to alleviate the suffering of those he left behind. He works with various Diaspora organizations, professionals, and human rights organizations to build a cross Atlantic alliance between Africans and international partners, promoting economic advancement, freedom, equality and justice in sub-Saharan Africa.

Dr. Ogula is the Director of Human Development and Special Programs at the largest Fire Department in the United States. In 2014, he was awarded the Leon Lowenstein Award, at the Fire Department of New York for continuing excellence, professionalism and executing human development programs. He has a doctorate degree in management and served as Professor, Vice President and Dean of the School of Business at

Apollos University; an educational evaluator for the Distance Education Accrediting Commission DEAC, and a consultant on emerging economies. His publications cover a range of topics including: Chaos Theory and Strategic Management, Attractors; Strange Attractors and Fractals; Corporate social responsibility, and various articles on social and political issues in Nigeria.

www.ingramcontent.com/pod-product-compliance
Lightning Source LLC
Chambersburg PA
CBHW021830020426
42334CB00014B/564